CREATE A
BEWITCHED FALL-O-WEEN

Published by

krause publications
An F&W Publications Company

700 East State Street • Iola, WI 54990-0001
715-445-2214 • 888-457-2873
www.krause.com

Please call or write for our free catalog of publications. Our toll-free number to place an order or obtain a free catalog is (800) 258-0929.

Library of Congress Catalog Number: 2003101370
ISBN: 0-87349-498-9

Edited by Maria L. Turner
Designed by Jan Wojtech

ACKNOWLEDGMENTS

We would like to thank the following friends, both old and new:

- SueAne Langdon, Jack Emrek, and Sherry Carlson for allowing us to invade and photograph their homes on more than one occasion.
- Sandy Hildebrandt and the StageCoach Inn Museum in Newbury Park, California, Michael Libow at the Witch's House in Beverly Hills, California, and Gary Blum at The Camarillo House and Barn in Camarillo, California, for allowing us to photograph at these locations, including shots for the cover.
- William and Meredith Asher for the childhood photograph of Elizabeth Montgomery.
- Maxine Fleckner Ducey and the University of Wisconsin at Madison for the childhood image of Agnes Moorehead.
- Krause Publications and our editor, Maria Turner as well as designers Jan Wojtech and Sharon Laufenberg.
- Alice Ghostley, a.k.a. Esmeralda of "Bewitched."
- Bernard Fox, a.k.a. Dr. Bombay of "Bewitched."
- Photographer David Skernick.
- Mike Kortan of Ohio.
- Mitch Watkins and Vincent Wilson at Hollywood Forever Memorial Park in Hollywood, California.
- Mr. and Mrs. Michael Maschet for the Vampire Wine.
- Kinko's Copy Stores.
- Dover Clip Art Books.

TABLE OF CONTENTS

AUTUMN FALLS - 7

AUTUMN AU-RRANGEMENTS - 17

CANDY CORN SHRINE - 31

HALLOWEEN HARKENS - 41

Well, here it is again: That crisp, colorful, somewhat creepy time of year. It's when the earth puts on her best gown for one last hurrah and parades her baubles all about the countryside.

In the following pages, Kasey and I will show you how you can utilize our world's best fall flora and fauna to illuminate your home for the season. Everything from some quick-fix Autumn Au-rangements, using many things right out of the backyard to a Green Goblin Get-Together, complete with all the accessories for a Halloween party right in your living room.
Think vintage and retro, as all those things from yesteryear never fail to evoke fond memories of autumns gone by. Stir in freshly fallen leaves, a heaping helping of plump pumpkins, a pilgrim, and a witch or two, and you've got a fun new season we like to call fall-o-ween.

Mark

Sheesh, Kasey. How many more quilts and suitcases do we really need for this photo shoot?

AUTUMN FALLS

As September draws to a close, it is time to get that autumn décor placed beautifully throughout your home. These decorative Wooden Band Boxes are just one of the projects in this section that will help set the scene. Here, we have filled them with good old-fashioned apples (in green and red), popcorn balls, and a mixture of nuts.

Autumn's Main Man

Let's hear it for fall's festive leader. Unlike most scarecrows that just sort of hang around, our straw-filled friend is coming right at you with arms flailing. In the immortal words of Dorothy: "Why, if the scarecrows back in Kansas could do that, the crows would be scared to pieces."

Scarecrows have been serving man for thousands of years. Standing guard on their lonely vigils night after night, they protect whatever crops might lie before them. Mention of them has even been found as far back as Ancient Egypt (although judging from their drawings and paintings, we're not too sure they wore very much). We chose to put our version of this fine fall fellow in a bit of a 1700s look, after finding a tricorn hat and corduroy knee britches hiding in some old Halloween stuff. And, we found the brown leather coat at a thrift store for less than $8.

Materials

- Polystyrene wig head form with molded features
- 8-oz. bottle Stiffy Fabric Stiffener by Plaid
- 18" string, yarn, or twine
- 1 yard muslin or other "hop-sacking" material
- 3 yards heavy jute rope
- 1 package long raffia
- 1/8-yard black broadcloth
- 2-oz. bottle Rusty Orange Delta Ceramcoat Acrylic Paint
- Brown powdered eye shadow
- 2 2¹/2"-wide x 8 feet-long tree stakes, pointed on one end (or 2" x 2" wood pieces 8 feet long)
- 13" x 2" x 2" piece scrap wood
- 5" x 1" metal plate
- 2 small screws
- 6" x ¹/4" bolt with nut
- Large metal bowl
- Old clothes of choice (We used corduroy knickers, hat, and old leather overcoat.)
- 1 pair suspenders
- Enough fabric scraps or bunched-up newspaper to stuff pants
- Serrated knife
- Scissors
- 1 package quilt pins
- 1 package greening pins
- Paintbrush
- Drill with 1¹/2" and ³/8" bits
- 2 4"-long nails
- Hammer
- Several safety pins
- Wood excelsior, moss, wheat, corn husks
- Newspaper
- Measuring tape
- Pencil
- Sewing machine and thread

Preparing the head:

1. Use serrated knife to cut a "V" shaped mouth into the polystyrene wig head, as shown at left.

2. After muslin has been washed and dried, tear ¹/4-yard off one end and set aside.

3. Once you have covered work area with newspaper, put Stiffy into a large bowl and dip large piece of muslin into the fabric stiffener until thoroughly saturated. Remove saturated muslin and place over wig head face.

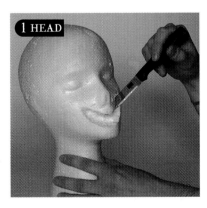

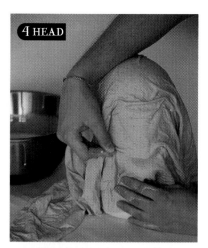

4 HEAD

4. Smooth fabric into cutout mouth and around nose and eyes until face is clearly defined, as shown at left.

5. To make his **malicious** leer, push the fabric up at the sides of the mouth, and then push down between eyes onto center of nose to cause a scowl. Hold wrinkles in place with quilt pins until dry.

6. Smooth muslin eye and nose area again, adding more Stiffy if needed. Use more pins to hold muslin in place.

7. Smooth muslin over rest of head and use string tied around neck to secure fabric.

8. Trim away excess fabric from around neck and allow head to dry.

Finishing the head:

1. Once the muslin is dry, remove the quilt pins and use the orange paint to color in a triangular nose.

2. Use the brown eye shadow to slightly darken the eye areas and face wrinkles.

3. Run a gathering stitch along one end of remaining ¼-yard piece of muslin.

4. Gather muslin and wrap around neck to form the collar. Tie off thread.

5. Wrap the rope around his neck two or three times and knot. Fray the ends.

6. Center the middle of the raffia onto his head, a little back of the forehead to give him a bit of a receding hairline. Hold in place with greening pins where his center "part" would be.

7. Tie hair into long ponytail with black broadcloth. Trim raffia shorter, if needed.

For the body:

1. Measure up 5 feet from pointed end of each tree stake, mark lightly with pencil, and drill ⅜" hole at pencil mark on each to accommodate ¼" x 6" bolt.

2. Bolt together in "X" shape and secure with wing-nut, as shown.

3. While poles can still be moved, completely dress scarecrow before continuing. First, slip on the pants and then coat.

1 BODY

2 BODY

3 BODY

Haunted HINT

There is no need to stuff the coat since the wood pole fills arms sufficiently enough to still allow for the arms to flap freely in the wind. But, do beat that old coat up a bit by washing it with a little bleach and hitting with a metal meat tenderizer on the pavement.

4. Measure 18" above bolt on each stake for placement of the crossbar, mark each with pencil, and while keeping clothing out of the way, drill hole into side of each pole and push 4" nail into hole.

6 BODY

5. Hammer nail into each end of 13" crossbar. Frame should now be rigid.

6. Screw 5" metal plate to middle of crossbar so that it protrudes above the crossbar, as shown at right.

7. Measure the distance between the two pointed ends of the stakes and and dig two 12" deep holes in the ground.

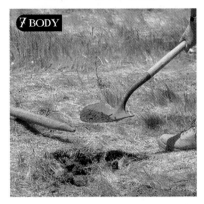
7 BODY

8. Stand scarecrow up, pointed ends in holes. Poles should reach about 7 feet in height. Fill holes with dirt and pack down for solid base.

9. Stuff scarecrow with excess fabric scraps or bunched newspaper, starting with the pants.

10. When sufficiently stuffed full, tie off pant legs with rope.

11. Clip suspenders to back of the stuffed pants, slip them underneath the coat and over the crossbar, and then snap them to the front of the pants.

12. Embellish the body with wooden excelsior, moss, weeds, cornhusks, and wheat sticking out from the ends of sleeves and pant legs. Cover the open top of the trousers with more of the same. Tuck the moss and excelsior into pockets and around the neck. No need to be neat since this guy needs to look like he's been moldering away in a field for a long time.

13. Slip polystyrene wig base onto 5" metal plate.

14. Pin hat securely to the top of his head.

Haunted HINT

Our jubilant hay-filled friend is visited by all sorts of critters, including large black crows sold in craft stores this time of year (near right). Patches made from colored felt squares and boldly stitched onto your scarecrow's clothes, along with a few silk flowers such as poppies or sunflowers tucked here and there, are great for an added dash of color. And if you don't have a pair of knickers to begin with, you can make a pair for your scarecrow by cutting off the legs of an old pair of trousers just below the knee. Use the leftover fabric to make a band and gather the pant leg to it. Then add a button and buttonhole so they close on the outside of each leg, as shown in far right photograph.

Candy Apples

STEP BACK IN TIME TO ANOTHER FALL FAVORITE AND INTRODUCE YOUR CHILDREN TO WONDERFUL CANDY APPLES. DELICIOUS, CRUNCHY, CANDY COVERED RED OR GREEN APPLES ON A STICK.

MATERIALS

- 10 candy/caramel apple sticks
- 10 firm red or green apples
- 1 package Sugar Crafts Candy Apple Magic Mix*
- 5 lbs. granulated sugar
- 2 c. water
- Candy thermometer
- Heavy saucepan and wooden spoon
- Greased cookie sheet
- Candy apple wrap

*We opted to make 10 candy apples, but the full recipes from Candy Apple Magic Mix will make 20 or 30.

1. Add contents of Candy Apple Magic Mix bag to 5 pounds of granulated sugar and 2 cups water. Make sure mix and sugar are dissolved before boiling starts. Insert candy thermometer and be sure to stir often.

2. While mixture is heating, de-stem the apples and push or tap wooden apple sticks into the top of each .

3. When thermometer reaches 290 to 300 degrees, turn heat off and begin dipping each apple. If mix cools down, reheat to about 300 degrees.

4. After dipping, tap apples to remove excess candy. Place on greased cookie sheet to cool.

5. When cool, wrap each apple in candy apple wrap.

The Old Dutch Church in Sleepy Hollow, New York, has been the infamous resting place for Washington Irving's Headless Horseman for almost two centuries. Built in 1697 by Frederick Philips, the church itself has been in continual use except during times of revolution. We visited the site, but didn't hang around long enough for nightfall, just in case hooves started pounding. Luckily, old Ichabod Crane's bridge still stands nearby.

Wooden Band Boxes

Wooden band boxes have been used for centuries to ship all kinds of goods in. By using wood veneer strips on papier-mache hatboxes, you can achieve a very similar look to the originals.

3 SMALL

6 SMALL

Haunted HINT

If the banding goes off-kilter, you may try pulling it up once, but after that, the sticky on the back will give up the ghost, so make sure it's in a good place to start. If the stickiness does fail, all is still not lost since the wood hot glue will make the strip useable again. Another fix for banding that has gone astray is to make a small snip in the banding and overlap where a star or heart will cover it.

MATERIALS

- 3 graduated papier-mâché hatboxes from Rusty Tin-tiques
- 3 packages Van Dyke's Walnut Flat-Cut Veneer Edge Banding
- 3 packages Van Dyke's Mahogany Flat-Cut Veneer Edge Banding
- 72 small wooden hearts
- 30 small wooden stars
- 26 little wooden bats
- 1 can clear spray varnish
- Hot glue gun and glue sticks for wood
- Pencil
- Scissors
- 1 to 3 drawer pulls (optional)

For the small box:

1. With the lid on the smallest box, use a pencil to draw a line around the base of lid and entire perimeter of box. Remove lid.

2. Measure around the box with a piece of mahogany wood veneer edge banding and cut the stripping that length.

3. Peel away just a bit of the protective paper backing from the banding, and starting just slightly under the drawn pencil line on the box, as shown at left, begin to press banding down lightly, peeling as you go.

4. Repeat steps 2 and 3 with the other color banding, placing it just below the first.

5. Trim the dark strip flush with the bottom of the box.

6. Use hot glue gun (filled with wood glue sticks) to attach wooden stars over the seam of where the mahogany and walnut bands meet, as shown.

7. For the lid, simply glue alternating strips of the wood veneer to the top and followed up with a band of wood veneer around the edge. Trimming it with scissors to fit.

8. Allow the adhesive on the backs of the strips to dry for 24 hours and then spray with a couple of coats of clear varnish.

9. If interested, screw a drawer pull to the lid, keeping it tight to the box with washers.

For the medium-sized box:

1. Follow step 1 from the instructions for the smallest box.

2. Now instead of measuring the veneer banding around the box, measure the length from the pencil line to the bottom of the box so that the strips may be place vertically.

3. Use the scissors to cut each veneer band to length.

4. Then place veneer bands vertically in the same manner explained in step 3 of the small box instructions, starting with mahogany and alternating with the walnut until the entire box is covered.

5. Measure around the box with a piece of mahogany wood veneer edge banding and cut the stripping that length.

6. Peel away just a bit of the protective paper backing from the banding, and finish off the box by placing this strip horizontally around the bottom edge of the box. Trim flush with the bottom of the box as necessary.

7. Complete the lid banding as in step 7 of the small box instructions (previous page).

8. When lid banding is completed, hot glue wooden bats around the lower edge of the lid, as shown at right.

9. Finish with clear varnish as in step 8 of the small box instructions (previous page).

For the large box:

1. Complete in the same manner as the small box, following steps 1 through 4 of the instructions (previous page).

2. After the walnut strip is placed, follow with another mahogany strip around the bottom and trim the final strip flush with the bottom of the box.

3. Use hot glue gun (filled with wood glue sticks) to attach wooden hearts over both the top and bottom seams of where the mahogany and walnut bands meet, as shown at right.

4. Complete large box in the same manner as outlined in steps 7 and 8 of the small box instructions (previous page).

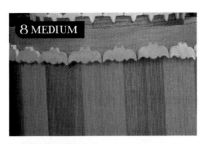

8 MEDIUM

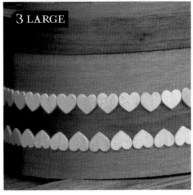

3 LARGE

Haunted HINT

A word of warning: If you decide to wrap your box with the wood stripping, as we have done on two of them, it is very easy to get slightly off-course as neither the boxes nor the wood stripping is exactly perfect. Keep in mind the wood stripping will curve but not bend.

These vintage-looking, hand-painted wooden signs of the times can be found at Island Moon online. Check out Resources, page 127, to order Mandy's wonderful old-time designs.

Beer Label Band Box

ANOTHER DECORATIVE METHOD FOR CREATING PRETTY FINISHED BOXES IS USING BEER AND WINE LABELS TO COVER THEM. BE SURE TO USE LABELS THAT REFLECT THE SEASON, INCLUDING THOSE FROM VAMPIRE WINE, PUMPKIN ALE, WICKED RED, AND OLD PECULIAR ALE.

MATERIALS

- 12"-diameter papier-mâché hatbox from Rusty Tin-tiques
- 15 beer and wine labels (at least three different kinds)
- 8-oz. bottle Stiffy Fabric Stiffener by Plaid
- Scissors
- Large metal bowl
- Color copier or home computer, scanner, and color printer

1. Photocopy labels on a color laser copier at your local copy center, or if you prefer, scan your labels using your computer and print them out in color.

2. Cut all labels out.

3. Pour Stiffy into bowl (slightly dilute with water, if needed).

4. Begin dipping each label into mixture and apply them to box and lid, overlapping as you go, until completely covered. Let dry.

Detail of Beer Label Band Box.

Haunted HINT

We soaked our beer bottles in warm water before removing the labels so that removal was much easier and the labels came off in a much better state for reproduction. Once you have them off the bottles, let them dry overnight before photocopying them. As for the number of photocopies needed, the exact count of labels will vary with the size of your box, but we made five copies of each of eight different varieties for a total of 40 labels.

AUTUMN AU-RRANGEMENTS

Following is a host of quick and simple tabletop "pretties" that will liven up any autumn table. These arrangements can work for Halloween as well by just carving the pumpkins.

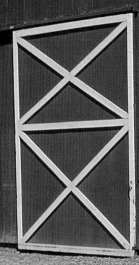

Antique Lamp Holders

THESE ANTIQUE LAMP BRACKETS ONCE SERVED A MUCH-NEEDED
PURPOSE. IN THE "OLDEN DAYS," THEY HELD KEROSENE LAMPS UP
HIGH AND COULD BE SWIVELED BACK AND FORTH TO SHED THE
LIGHT ALL ABOUT. TODAY, THEY MAKE IDEAL PLANT HOLDERS,
CANDLEHOLDERS, OR CLEVER PLACES FOR NICE ARRANGEMENTS
LIKE THE ONE WE CREATED HERE. ALTHOUGH WE CHOSE TO
HANG OURS OUTSIDE ATTACHED TO A TREE, YOU MAY HANG
YOURS INSIDE INSTEAD.

MATERIALS

- 1 pair reproduction lamp brackets*
- 1 small pie-pumpkin
- 2 bunches real or artificial red grapes
- 1 package Spanish moss
- 1 package quilt pins

- 6 autumn leaves
- 3 baby's breath sprigs

*We obtained our brackets from Tender Heart Treasures (Resources, page 128)

1. Place a small wreath of moss in the bottom of the bracket's holder, as shown at right (1A and 1B).

2. Place pumpkin on top of the moss and use quilt pins to attach the grapes by their stems to the pumpkin's base.

3. Hide quilt pins with baby's breath and brightly colored leaves tucked securely into the arrangement.

Above, detail of finished Antique Lamp Holders.

Candles-In-a-Compote

Glass Christmas balls come in a rainbow
of colors these days, including many
autumn shades. They add an elegant touch
of beauty to this project and are easily
found through Krebs (Resources, page 127).
Let your imagination run!

MATERIALS

- Crystal compote*
- Pillar candle
- 6 burgundy glass balls
- 6 orange glass balls
- 6 gold-tone glass balls
- Earthquake putty or museum wax
- 6 Plastic Foam 3-D Stars
- 1 tube orange glitter
- 1 tube brown glitter (or red)
- White glue
- Disposable 1" paintbrush
- Newspaper

*Be aware that the size of your compote may cause some variation in the number of glass balls and 3-D stars needed.

1. Place a tall pillar candle in crystal compote. (If the candle appears to be too short, raise it by setting it on an overturned glass.)

2. Add the autumn-colored glass balls to the compote, around the base of the candle, as shown at right. If you find the glass balls just won't stay where you want them, add a bit of earthquake putty or museum wax to the underside.

3. Spread newspaper over a flat work surface and lay out the stars. Be sure to have glitter bottles open and ready to use.

4. Use the paintbrush to give a very light coating of glue to one side of the stars.

5. Sprinkle each star evenly with glitter until completely encrusted and allow to dry.

6. Repeat steps 4 and 5 for other side.

7. When dry, tuck the stars in and around the balls and candle.

Haunted HINT

Look in antique stores or your own family albums for Victorian-era photographs of elderly women. These instant ancestors lend a quaint and charming touch when framed in ornate silver frames or just tucked into arrangements. (We won't mention how much ours resemble… well, you know, the "Broomstick Set.")

Good friend, SueAne Langdon, whom many will remember singing along with Elvis in movies such as "Roustabout" and "Frankie and Johnny," lights up the Glass Pumpkin Bowls for a sparkling Halloween celebration. See the next page for an overview on this variation to the Candles-In-a-Compote project.

For a variation to the Candles-in-a-Compote project on the previous page, try using red grapes instead of the glass Christmas balls. And to make this variation a bit more fall-o-weenish, fill small glass ivy bowls with water that has been dyed with eight drops of yellow food coloring and one drop of red. Cut out small, black felt triangles, and tape them to the front of each bowl to resemble the face of a jack-o-lantern. Add a floating candle for the final glowing effect.

Glass Pumpkin Bowls

Rusted Urn and Metal Star Candleholders

The highly sought-after Monterey style of furniture collected by Sue Ane Langdon and her husband Jack Emrek makes for a perfect backdrop to many of our Autumn Au-rrangements, including this Rusted Urn and Metal Star Candleholders project.

MATERIALS

- 1 Modern Options Rusting Kit
- 1 small metal urn
- 1 bunch raffia
- 1" paintbrush
- 2 rusted metal "beam" stars from old buildings
- 2 wood candle cups
- 1 small pie-pumpkin
- 2 tall taper candles
- 1 package moss
- Hot glue gun and glue sticks

1. "Rust" the urn and wooden candle cups according to Modern Options package instructions.

2. Hot glue the candle cups to the middle of the stars.

3. Hot glue the moss randomly on the urn to give it an aged look.

4. Add candles to stars and place pumpkin on top of urn.

5. Tie pumpkin with a small raffia bow.

6. Artfully hot glue bits of moss to top of pumpkin and around top of urn, as shown at left.

Haunted HINT

You may wish to put little felt "feet" on the bottoms of the stars and urn, so that the rust will not come off on your furniture and fine linens.

Vintage Hanky Inspiration

OLD HANKIES CAN BE FOUND IN VINTAGE AND ANTIQUE STORES, NOT TO MENTION ALL OVER EBAY. LET THE GREAT OLD GRAPHICS INSPIRE YOUR COLOR SCHEME AND ARRANGEMENT. OUR HANKY IS WHITE, CREAM, BROWN, AND GREEN—NOT YOUR USUAL AUTUMN SHADES BUT STILL PERFECT. LITTLE FLOWERS AND OAK LEAVES ARE PRINTED ON IT, SO WE JUST HAD TO FIND A WAY TO MAKE IT ALL WORK.

1. Place cake stand in center of table and drape handkerchief over the top, as shown below.

2. Remove oak leaves from the twigs and pin decoratively to the top of the pumpkin.

3. Break bunches of baby's breath into smaller pieces and tuck randomly around the oak leaves and stem on top of the pumpkin, as shown bottom right.

4. Finish by simply placing a few more bunches of baby's breath tucked underneath the pumpkin on top of the cake stand and then one more bunch on the tabletop decoratively around the cake stand foot.

MATERIALS

- Square china cake stand
- Vintage handkerchief
- White pumpkin
- 2 oak tree twig cuttings with leaves
- 3 bunches baby's breath
- Several quilt pins

Paper Leaf Wreath

MATERIALS

- 10" straw wreath
- 4 packages
  Black Ink Paper Leaves
- 1 package small straight pins
- Three-wick pillar candle
  (optional)

Paper Leaf Wreath with a candle in the center as a pretty variation to hanging it.

THIS VERSATILE FALL WREATH CAN BE USED IN A NUMBER OF WAYS, INCLUDING HANGING ON A WALL OR AS A RING FOR A LARGE, THREE-WICK CANDLE. JUST BE CAREFUL WHEN USING THE CANDLE VARIATION WITH SUCH EASILY FLAMMABLE MATERIALS AS THE PAPER LEAVES AND STRAW WREATH.

1. Begin pinning the leaves to the wreath in a slight overlapping way, making sure they extend well over the side. Continue until you have used all four packages.

2. Hang on a door, or place on flat surface with candle in the center, as shown at left.

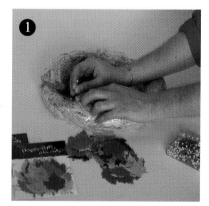

Haunted HINT

If you plan to use the wreath from year to year, you will want to secure the leaves with hot glue. In our case, we used the wreath for just one season and the assembly with the pins allowed us to simply remove them and use all the project components for other projects.

As noted earlier in this book, glass ornaments aren't just for Christmas anymore. Such well-known designers as Christopher Radko are creating them in shapes for Halloween, Easter, and even St. Patrick's Day (see Resources, page 127). Here, we utilize an owl ornament on a branch to create a unique piece to adorn a corner of any room.

What-a-Hoot

Materials

- Tarnished silver pitcher or vase
- Clip-on owl ornament
- Shapely dry branch
- 3 to 5 twigs colorful fall leaves
- 1 package reindeer moss
- 1 block Floracraft dry foam
- Hot glue gun and glue sticks

1. Wedge the dry foam into the pitcher.
2. Insert dried twigs into the foam and secure with hot glue, if needed.
3. Tuck in touches of the reindeer moss.
4. Accent the arrangement with a bright owl ornament clipped on near the center.

These vintage electric stars were originally used as Christmas tree toppers. In fact, one has adorned Mark's tree since birth. But with the addition of some fall foliage and pumpkins, these stars aren't just for Christmas anymore. Mix in some vintage childhood photos for an arrangement that will last the entire season.

Speaking of childhood photos. Can you name the famous witches that appear in ours? See page 128 for the answers.

Stars of Halloween

Bloomin' Boots

Lace-up granny boots were all the rage in the 1980s and can sometimes still be found in shoe stores, outlets, and thrift stores. Today, they are the perfect container for a crisp autumn bouquet of sunflowers and baby's breath.

MATERIALS

- 10 large sunflowers
- 1 bunch baby's breath
- 1 bunch large green leaves from root vegetables
- 1 large garlic bud
- 2 large red or purple root vegetables
- 4 large twist ties
- 3 lbs. small metal weights or sand
- 2 empty 8-oz. Parmesan cheese plastic containers
- Red food coloring

1. Place sunflower stems in a large bucket of water. Add at least 20 drops red food coloring until water is crimson. Leave flowers in water overnight or until flowers have absorbed the coloring and become tinged with red, as shown.

2. Place approximately 1½ pounds of weight in the toe/bottom of each boot using the metal weights or sand.

3. Fill empty Parmesan containers half full of red water.

4. Put one water-filled container in each of the boots and lace-up around it.

5. Gather five sunflowers into an artistic arrangement and wrap stems with twist ties to help hold their shape. Repeat for second bouquet.

6. Tuck large green leaves in around top of boots.

7. Insert one flower arrangement into water in each boot.

8. Round out each arrangement by tucking baby's breath into spaces.

9. On the table, add a couple of colorful root vegetables, leaves, and a large bud of garlic to complete the display, as shown.

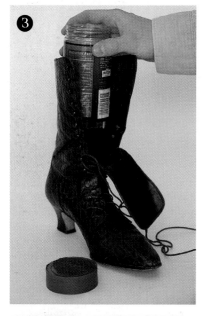

CANDY CORN SHRINE

Candy Corn: Autumn's most well-known treat now gets a celebration all its own with the projects presented throughout this section.

Candy Corn Topiaries

The typical shape of a topiary tree lends itself perfectly to the shape of the candy corn. So, here is a great project to serve as centerpiece on a dining table or a decorative flair on an end table or mantle.

MATERIALS

- 3 4" x 15" polystyrene cones
- Delta Ceramcoat
  Acrylic Paint
  - 2-oz. bottle yellow
  - 2-oz. bottle orange
  - 2-oz. bottle ivory
  - 2-oz. bottle black
- 1 tube Creative Beginnings
  Gold Ultra Fine
  Diamond Dust Glitter
- 3 4½" clay pots
- 2 ¾" x 44" wooden dowels
- 2 blocks Floracraft Dry Foam
- 3¾ yards black gimp
- 3 1"-diameter black pompons
- 1 bag sheet moss
- 12 or more
  colorful fall leaves
- Paintbrush
- Scissors
- Handsaw
- Hot glue gun and glue sticks

For the two matching topiary trees:

1. Cut two polystyrene cones into three pieces each: bottom at 3½" tall, middle at 7" tall, and top at 4½" tall.

2. Paint bottom section yellow and while paint is still wet, sprinkle with glitter.

3. Paint the middle section orange and top section ivory and sprinkle with glitter while each is wet, just as for the bottom section in step 2.

4. When dry, measure and cut gimp lengths to fit around the top and bottom of both the yellow and orange sections and around the bottom of the ivory section.

5. Hot glue the gimp pieces to the appropriate edges of each section.

6. Using the handsaw, cut wooden dowels into pieces as follows:

- three 8" lengths
- two 6" lengths
- two 4" lengths

7. Paint doweling black and allow to dry.

8. Wedge dry foam into clay pots, filling to the top. Poke a hole in the top of the foam with doweling.

9. Use dowel to then poke holes centered in the bottom of ivory section, and the bottoms and tops of orange and yellow sections. Adjust depth of holes to allow for proper space of doweling between sections.

10. Fill holes with hot glue and reinsert dowels, building the topiary from the pot up. The 8" dowel is on the bottom, 6" is next, and the 4" is used last. Be careful to line up the black doweling vertically so your topiary is straight.

11. Hot glue moss to cover foam base on each tree

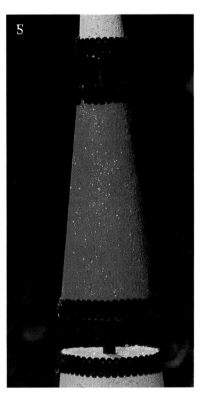

12. Hot glue three colorful leaves in the moss, as shown below.

13. Hot glue pompon to top of each tree, as shown.

Single Candy Corn Tree:

1. Do not cut polystyrene cone.

2. Paint and glitter according to steps 2 and 3 in the previous instructions.

3. Measure and cut gimp length to fit around the bottom and where each of the colors meet.

4. Hot glue gimp pieces in place.

5. Hot-glue pompon to top of tree.

6. Fill the clay pot with dry foam as in step 8 of the matching topiary instructions on the previous page.

7. Insert one of the remaining 8" piece of doweling into center of dry foam and center of the bottom of embellished cone.

8. Remove dowel, fill holes with hot glue, and reinsert doweling to create topiary.

9. Hot glue moss to cover dry foam.

10. Glue three colorful leaves into moss.

Haunted HINT

Tiny topiaries can be made using a toothpick, real piece of candy corn, and a miniature clay pot. Add a bit of dry foam to the pot, insert toothpick into candy corn, and then into dry foam. Cover foam with a bit of moss. Be aware that sometimes the candy corn will break. In that case, you will have to eat that piece and start over. Isn't crafting with candy rough?

Candy Corn Under Glass

Glass-covered candy jars are a hot collectible these days, so we've decided to create a new use for them: to serve dessert. Use small ones for individual servings and larger ones for "dessert-for-two." They can often be collected from thrift stores.

Haunted HINT

Do not add fresh or canned pineapple to gelatin. It will not gel appropriately for this project.

MATERIALS

- 6 small glass or crystal compotes with lids
- 6-oz. package pineapple or lemon gelatin
- 6-oz. package orange gelatin
- 7 c. water
- 2 8-oz. tubs whipped topping
- 8 to 10 drops yellow food coloring
- half-can mandarin orange segments, well drained
- 1 can non-dairy whipped topping

For yellow layer:

1. Prepare gelatin according to directions on box, but reduce water by ½ cup.

2. Refrigerate approximately one-and-a-half hours or until thickened.

3. Whip one tub of whipped topping into gelatin.

4. If not yellow enough, add drops of yellow food coloring to reach desired color.

5. Fill compotes one-quarter full with yellow mixture.

6. Chill until firm and then continue with orange layer.

For orange layer:

1. Repeat steps 1 through 3 as in the yellow layer above.

2. When the gelatin-whipped topping mixture is cool and thick, fold in mandarin oranges.

3. Spoon the orange mixture over yellow layer until compote is three-quarters full.

4. Chill until set.

5. At serving time add non-dairy topping to top one-quarter of compote and also fill tops, as shown above left.

The finished creation, at left, is a delicious and fun dessert to match your candy corn-themed linens and accessories.

Candy Corn Table Topper

Set the mood of your get-together with a
felt tablecloth of candy corn colors. Felt is
an inexpensive and easy-to-use medium that
is really popular in home decorating right
now, so you will look chic without spending
a lot of money.

MATERIALS

- ½-yard 36"-wide cream-colored felt
- 2 yards 36"-wide orange felt
- 2 yards 36"-wide yellow felt
- 1 spool each of thread in matching colors: cream, orange, and yellow
- 1½ yards 54"-wide ivory lining fabric
- Sewing machine
- Newspaper
- Scissors or rotary cutter
- Iron
- Ruler or measuring tape

For the paper pattern:

1. Tape newspaper together into a 56" x 36" rectangle, as shown at left.

2. Fold newspaper with the fold measuring 36", as shown.

3. Measure up 26" from bottom and mark, as shown below.

4. Draw a straight line from the 26" mark out to the lower corner, as shown below.

5. Cut along line through all sheets of newspaper, creating a triangle.

6. With newspaper still folded, measure 7½" down from top along the fold line and mark. Then, measure 8½" up from bottom and mark. Draw lines from both marks across the pattern, as shown below.

1 PAPER

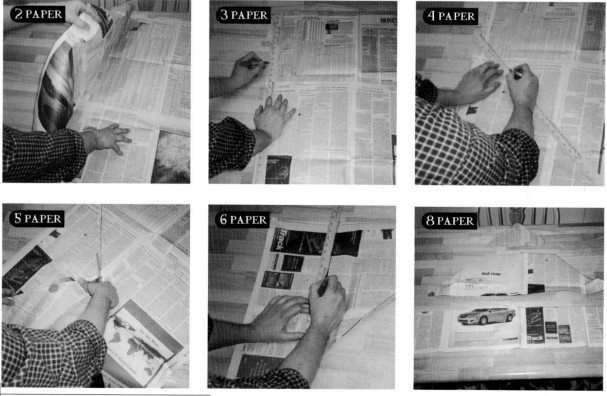

2 PAPER 3 PAPER 4 PAPER

5 PAPER 6 PAPER 8 PAPER

7. Cut through both layers of paper along the drawn lines.

8. Unfold each pattern piece as your guide for cutting the felt pieces, as shown on previous page.

For the table topper itself:

1. Using the newspaper patterns and being careful so that the ink does not rub off onto the felt, cut the following:

- four top pieces from the cream-colored felt
- four middle pieces from the orange felt
- four bottom pieces from the yellow felt

2. With ½" seam allowance, stitch a cream-colored top felt piece to a middle orange felt piece, and then stitch both to a bottom yellow felt piece. Repeat for the other three sides.

3. Press all seams open flat. Using matching thread, topstitch all seams flat. Repeat for other three sides.

4. Stitch all triangles together to form a square table topper. Again press all seams open flat and topstitch using the yellow thread.

5. Lay candy corn topper flat, right-side down onto lining fabric. Pin all edges and stitch around perimeter leaving a 6" "turn hole" on one side (never at a corner).

6. Turn entire piece right side out and press.

7. Topstitch around entire perimeter with yellow thread, catching turn hole edge.

Detail of finished table topper.

Drink It All In

Fill a martini glass whose stem is made in matching colors with more candy corn to add yet another embellishment to your themed table.

Candy Corn Napkins

HOMEMADE NAPKINS ARE A GREAT (AND INEXPENSIVE) WAY TO DRESS UP YOUR TABLETOP AND FRESHEN THE LOOK OF PLAIN LINENS THAT HAVE BEEN USED BEFORE. THESE ARE A SNAP FOR EXPERIENCED SEWERS, BUT ALSO ARE EASY ENOUGH FOR THE NOVICE.

MATERIALS

(makes nine 14" napkins)
- 1⅛ yards 45"-wide candy corn print fabric
- Thread
- Scissors or rotary cutter
- Sewing machine
- Iron

1. Cut fabric into nine 15" squares.

2. Press all four sides in ¼" and then another ¼" making all raw edges internal.

3. Machine stitch all four sides of each napkin using ⅛" seam allowance.

4. Use iron to press again before displaying on your table.

Haunted HINT

If you'd like lined napkins, see pages 55-56 under Green Goblin Get-Together.

HALLOWEEN HARKENS

The ghostly colors of silver, crystal, and white used in this table setting really scare up visions of a haunted evening. Of interest to "Bewitched" fans: The portrait of Kasey in the green sequin gown was a prop used in an episode where Darrin (played by Dick Sargent in this case) paints Louise Tate's picture. For more on this famous prop portrait, look ahead to the Green Goblin Get-Together, page 49.

Silvered Pumpkin

THOSE PLASTIC TRICK-OR-TREAT PUMPKINS WE ALL GREW UP WITH
(THOSE UNDER THE AGE OF 50, THAT IS) ARE ABOUT TO TAKE ON A
NEW LIFE WITH DELTA RENAISSANCE FOIL KITS. TURN THAT TACKY
PLASTIC PUMPKIN INTO A TREASURED "SCARELOOM."

MATERIALS

- Plastic pumpkin
- 2 Delta Silver Renaissance Foil Kits
- 7 to 10 dried weeds and leaves
- 1 brick Floracraft Dry Foam
- Aluminum foil
- 1 can black spray paint
- 1 can Design Masters silver spray paint
- 1 tube Creative Beginnings Green Ultra Fine Diamond Dust Glitter
- Newspaper

1. Spray paint the pumpkin with the silver spray paint and let dry.

2. Follow the package instructions on the Delta Renaissance Foil Kit to silver the pumpkin and let dry.

3. Spread some newspaper outside and spray paint the weeds and leaves black. Allow painted pieces to dry.

4. When dry, spray the leaves and weeds again and this time, while still wet, sprinkle them with the glitter.

5. Wrap the dry foam with the aluminum foil so that the foam will blend seamlessly with the finished pumpkin and push it inside the pumpkin.

6. Push each blackened weed stem into the foam to create a spectacular display.

HALLOWEEN *Hijinks*

Halloween is also known as "Nut Crack Night." An old superstition tells of tossing chestnuts onto a fire named for different lady friends or gentleman callers. The first to pop is the truest and the last, well, is not so interested. Other games of days gone by include making a King's Cake. Hidden within flour are trinkets that stand for love, matrimony, children, etc. The flour is tightly packed in a bowl, turned out on a tray, and made available for guests to cut a slice. Whatever ends up in their slice is what is in store for them in the coming year.

Notice how the Silvered Pumpkin is displayed wonderfully with the use of two cake stands topped with a black variation of the Lace Cake Stand Toppers, which are found on page 70.

Cloud Tablecloth

THIS TABLECLOTH MAY TAKE "VOLUMINOUS" YARDS OF FABRIC, BUT YOU CAN EASILY ROLL IT BACK UP WHEN DONE AND EITHER SAVE IT FOR ANOTHER PARTY OR USE IT TO MAKE SOMETHING ELSE.

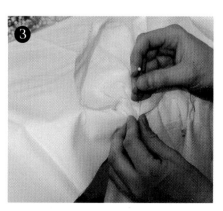

MATERIALS

- 8 yards 54"-wide white scrim fabric
- 1 package quilt pins
- White beach towel
- Scissors or rotary cutter

1. Lay the towel open across the tabletop.

2. Cut 1 yard from the scrim and lay it across the towel to cover.

3. About 5" from one edge, begin gathering and pinning the rest of the scrim to the towel at the table's edge. Be sure the pins point downward and are well-seated into the fabric.

4. Tuck excess fabric under the table in a blouson effect.

Black Widow's Delight

The things you can make out of a box cake these days—just scary! With the simple addition of food coloring, frozen blackberries, and friendly spiders, you don't have to work hard to scare up this Halloween party treat.

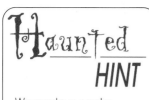

Haunted HINT

We made our cake three ultimate layers of yummy-ness. With the leftover batter, we baked some cupcakes.

MATERIALS

- 2 boxes white cake mix
- 1 pint heavy whipping cream
- 1 package Ice Blue Island Twists Kool-Aid
- 2 bottles Sugar Craft Black Powdered Food Coloring (#5195)
- 1 package frozen blackberries
- 1 cup granulated sugar
- 1 box powdered sugar
- 3 round 9" cake pans
- 6 small plastic spiders
- Large freezer-safe bowl
- Large mixing bowl
- Electric beater

1. The night before baking the cake, put the frozen berries in a large bowl and sugar to taste with the granulated sugar. Leave in the fridge overnight. The berries will create tons of juice. Check periodically to see if they need more sugar.

2. Bake cake according to package instructions.

3. Pour the whipping cream into a large bowl and whip with electric beaters until it begins to thicken.

4. Add the packet of Kool-Aid and a bit of powdered sugar to the cream and whip some more.

5. Add one bottle (these are small bottles) of black powdered food coloring and whip a bit more.

6. Keep adding powdered sugar (to taste) and then add the other black food coloring bottle. Continue to whip until the cream is holding its own in fluffy black peaks.

7. Layer the cake pieces with the black whipped cream mixture and a few black berries.

8. Spread black whipped cream mixture on top and sides to cover decoratively.

9. Add berries to top, allowing the juice to rain down in rivulets to the plate. Serve remaining berries from a crystal dish set in a silver compote.

10. Embellish with plastic spiders.

A Nose for Halloween Fun

For the Silvered Pinocchio Masks above, see Kasey and Mark's book "Halloween Crafts: Eerily Elegant Décor" (Krause Publications). It has all the directions for these whimsical, yet elegant, face-hiders. If your local bookstore is sold out, try Amazon.com or buy directly from Krause at www.krause.com.

❾

To complete the look of this elegant table, mix in some solid white and clear glass Christmas balls by Krebs; white pumpkins; clear glass pumpkins (found in craft and florist shops); Java Lava black plates by Libbey; Vampire Wine's Pinot Grigio (see Resources, page 128); and all your best silver and crystal. And although you may want to wash the dust out of that crystal, don't bother to polish the silver. After all, it is Halloween. You have permission to use it tarnished. Take that, Emily Post!

A Pumpkin-Smashing Success

The last of the "Bewitched" gang got back together at Samantha and Darrin's house (top left) to start some new Halloween hi-jinks in the old neighborhood. In reality, the house, which still stands on a Hollywood back lot, is nothing more than a shell. If you look carefully, you can see that you wouldn't be able to stand up in the upstairs as the second story was only built three-quarter scale. Ah, the magic of Hollywood extends well past the floating props and disappearance acts performed on the show. Many thanks to our favorite witch and warlock Alice Ghostley (Esmeralda, right) and Bernard Fox (Dr. Bombay, above).

"Calling Dr. Bombay. Emergency: Come right away!"

GREEN GOBLIN GET-TOGETHER

Kasey's Halloween party this year featured a different color scheme than the typical orange and black of the season; it was chartreuse and black. Notice the picture on the wall of Kasey as Louise Tate from "Bewitched." How's that for a visit from a ghost from TV past?

Green Goblins

There was a time when these plastic pumpkins only came in orange. Today, they can be found in a multitude of shades from purple to fuchsia to black, and everything in between. We chose the chartreuse ones because of the eerie glow they cast with a light inside.

MATERIALS

- 10" plastic pumpkin bucket (color of choice)
- 1 yard ribbon (color to match pumpkin)
- 1 to 5 black silk roses with leaves*
- 1 to 5 silk roses (color to match pumpkin)
- ½-sheet poster board
- 11"-square scrap corrugated cardboard
- ½-yard 72"-wide black felt
- 3M Spray-Mount Adhesive
- Thrift store lamp base
- ⅛-yard 45"-wide unwashed top fabric (color/print to match pumpkin)
- ⅛-yard 45"-wide unwashed black decorative lining
- 25-watt lightbulb
- 1 can Design Masters High-Gloss Black Spray Paint
- Masking tape
- Black thread
- Needle
- X-Acto knife
- Scissors
- Hot glue gun and glue sticks
- Iron
- Straight pins
- Hat pattern (page 111)
- 6 8½" chartreuse pompons (optional)

*If black roses are difficult to find, spray paint any silk rose and its leaves using Design Masters spray paint. First, remove the leaves from the stem and lay them flat. Then, hold the rose by its stem and spray evenly.

For the hat:

1. Enlarge pattern of brim and hat patterns on pages 110-111 150% so you end up with one that is 12" tall.

2. Use the hat pattern to cut one poster board 12" cone and one matching black felt cone.

3. Use the brim pattern to cut one corrugated cardboard brim and two matching black felt brim pieces.

4. Spray the spray-mount adhesive onto one side of the corrugated cardboard brim.

5. Place one black felt brim piece onto the adhesive side of the cardboard brim and press firmly.

6. Repeat steps 4 and 5 for other side of the corrugated cardboard brim.

7. Trim outer edges of felt, if needed, and using small stitches, whipstitch the felt together, making sure to cover the cardboard edges of brim.

8. Whipstitch the inside felt brim edges as well, concealing the cardboard as you go.

9. Spray-mount black felt to dull side of the poster board hat cone in same manner as outlined in steps 4 and 5. Smooth out.

10. Roll felt-covered cone into the shape of the witch hat and pinch the point together, creasing the poster board.

11. Put needle and knotted thread through point starting on the uncovered poster board side.

12. While maintaining the cone shape, whipstitch with tiny stitches all the way down the back seam, catching the felt only.

13. When finished stitching, pinch point of cone back into desired shape.

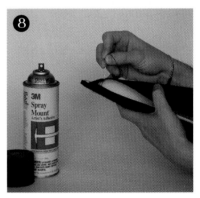

14. Slip brim over cone and down to proper level and then whipstitch it to the hat top.

15. Cut ends of ribbon into points and then wrap it around base of cone until top of ribbon is as taut as the bottom of ribbon. In back, cross ribbon ends over and stitch in place.

16. Hot glue one black rose and one smaller chartreuse rose to hide the stitches and add a couple of leaves. For the more elaborate hats, lavish the brims with more roses and leaves.

Above, detail of finished hat and below is detail of tie.

For the bow ties (yields all three):

1. Using unwashed fabric, cut three 5" x 30" strips of both top and lining fabrics for a total of six fabric pieces, three of each type.

2. Pin each top fabric strip to each lining fabric strip, right sides facing, and using a ½" seam allowance, stitch around the perimeter, leaving 3" turn-opening on one side (never at a corner).

3. Clip corners, turn right-side out, press, and set sewn-together strips aside.

4. For the knot fabric, cut three 5" squares from either fabric.

5. Using a fan fold, scrunch each piece of knot fabric until it is about 1½" wide and press to hold shape. Set aside.

6. Fold each long sewn-together strip into equal parts as shown at left and pinch together in the middle.

7. Pinch folded strip together in the middle, wrap knot fabric around middle as shown at left, and whipstitch in back.

8. Trim away any excess on knot.

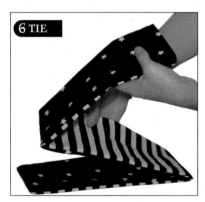

6 TIE

For the lamp bases:

1. Cover lamp base socket with masking tape.

2. Spray base with black Design Masters high-gloss enamel spray paint and let dry.

3. Add a second coat of spray paint, if necessary.

4. Let dry and remove tape.

7 TIE

Assembling the Green Goblins:

1. When lamp base is completely dry, remove light bulb or harp that may be attached to base and temporarily set aside.

2. Use an X-Acto knife to carefully cut a 3" x 3" X-shape in the bottom of green plastic pumpkin.

3. Work green plastic pumpkin down over the top of the lamp socket through the "X."

4. Add the light bulb back into the base, top the pumpkin with the felt witch hat, plug in, and switch them on.

Green Goblin Table Topper

TABLE TOPPERS AND NAPKINS ABOUND IN THIS BOOK, MOSTLY BECAUSE THEY ARE SO SIMPLE TO MAKE AND CAN CHANGE THE LOOK OF ANY DINING ROOM INTO A HOLIDAY EXTRAVAGANZA.

MATERIALS

- 1¼ yards 45"-wide top fabric (to match Goblin pumpkin)
- 1⅛ yards 45"-wide edging fabric (to match Goblin pumpkin)
- 1½ yards 54"-wide decorative lining (to complement top fabric)
- Scissors or rotary cutter
- Iron
- Straight pins
- Thread
- Sewing machine

1. Prewash and dry all fabrics.

2. From edging fabric, cut eight 5" x 45" bands.

3. With right sides together, stitch two bands end to end, thereby creating four 90" bands. Press seams open flat.

4. With right sides facing, center one strip on one side of 45" square top fabric piece. Be sure the band seam is in the middle of the topper and the ends extend way beyond the edges.

5. Pin strip in place and using a ½" seam allowance, stitch.

6. Repeat steps 4 and 5 for remaining three sides.

7. Once you have attached the edge strips to all four sides of the topper, press all seams inward toward center square, as shown (7A), clipping corners as needed so it will lay flat (7B).

8. Lay entire topper flat right-side up on worktable or floor, allowing the two side bands to lay *over* the top and bottom bands.

9. Fold overhang of a side band under itself, forming a 90-degree angle from the corner, press, and pin, as shown (9A and 9B).

10. Trim excess "tails" away from both strips, as shown.

11. Using matching thread, topstitch mitered corner very close to edge, as shown. Be sure to use a backstitch at beginning so thread won't pull out.

12. Repeat steps 9 and 10 for other three corners.

13. Press and cut away excess material under topper.

14. To line, place constructed topper on top of lining, right sides together. Pin around perimeter.

15. Using a ½" seam allowance, stitch top to lining, leaving a 6" turn-opening on one side (never on a corner).

16. Clip corners, turn, and press.

17. Whipstitch turn-opening closed.

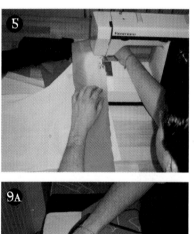

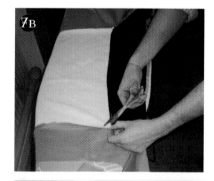

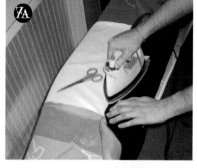

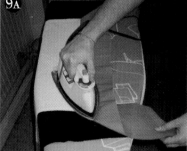

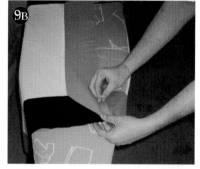

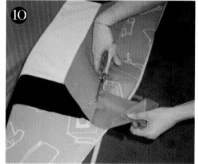

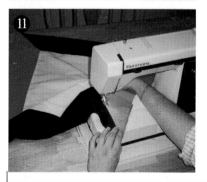

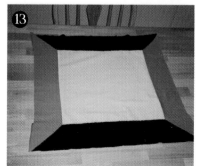

Note: The fabrics shown here in the how-to photos are for illustrative purposes only and do not match the actual fabrics used for this project.

Green Goblin Lined Napkins

WITH NO HEMMING REQUIRED, THESE LINED
NAPKINS ARE QUICK AND EASY TO MAKE. JUST BE
SURE TO WASH ALL FABRICS BEFORE STARTING AND
SELECT COMPLIMENTARY HALLOWEEN FABRICS. A
STRIPE IS ALWAYS EASY TO FOLLOW AND PERHAPS
A PRINT FOR THE LINING OR REVERSIBLE SIDE.

Detail of finished napkin above.

MATERIALS

- 1¼ yards primary fabric
- 1¼ yards lining fabric
- Scissors or rotary cutter
- Straight pins
- Needle
- Thread
- Sewing machine
- Measuring tape

1. Cut both the primary fabric and the lining fabric into 15" squares. You will end up with 12 squares in each fabric, or 24 squares total.

2. Place each primary fabric square right sides together with each lining square and pin in the corners.

3. Place a pin in the center to hold the two fabrics firmly together.

4. Starting at the center of one side, stitch ½" from edge. (Never start at a corner.)

5. Stitch all the way around the perimeter of each napkin, leaving a 2" turn-hole opening on the side where you started.

6. Clip all corners, turn right-sides out, and press.

7. Close turn-hole opening with small hand stitches, or machine topstitch all the way around just inside the ½" mark for a nice tailored look.

So Sweet It's Scary!

Lime green candy fruit slices and a small, green pumpkin candle take the cake. For cake recipe, see Black Widow's Delight, page 46.

HALLOWEEN *Hijinks*

Pulling kale (a bitter cabbage-type leaf) and staring in a mirror are great ways to tell who your true love really is.

For the first game, the fair maiden is blindfolded and led out into the garden patch (by moonlight, of course). She is instructed to tug on a piece of kale until it gives. If the stalk comes up easily, the sweetheart will be easy to win, if not... well, you know the rest. If dirt clings to the root, he will be rich, if the root is disfigured and hideous, look out! If the kale is taken home and hung over the doorway, the first person (outside of family) to pass under it will bear the same initials of the ultimately intended. As for the mirror game, which is depicted above in a graphic on a vintage Halloween postcard, a maiden must walk down the cellar stairs backwards while holding a candle in one hand and a mirror in the other. Upon reaching the bottom step, a smoky vision of her intended will appear. And who said living without TV in the Victorian age was no fun?

Ghoul Drool

THIS TART BUT YUMMY "GHOUL-AID" IS ALSO RATHER GHOUD FOR YOU. IT'S THE PERFECT NONALCOHOLIC DRINK TO SERVE AT ANY HALLOWEEN-RELATED EVENT, WHETHER IT BE A PARTY FOR THE KIDS OR THE ADULTS.

MATERIALS

- 6 green apples
- 12 scoops vanilla ice cream
- 6 c. seltzer water
- 1 c. plus 2 T. Fairies Finest Green Apple Sugar
- 6 decorative glasses
- 6 black straws
- 6 black plastic spiders
- Paring knife or apple corer
- Blender

1. Core apple but leave skin on and place in blender (up to three at a time can be done).

2. Add seltzer water, vanilla ice cream, and Green Apple Sugar.

3. Blend thoroughly.

4. Pour into glasses and top with another serving of vanilla ice cream and an icky black plastic spider.

Green Granny Smith apples in a black compote bowl make a fine centerpiece.

More Great Ideas

Kasey offers up a nice cool glass of Ghoul Drool. Drink if you dare!

Try filling vintage glass candy apothecary-type jars with jellybeans to match your color scheme. With all the wild new flavors out today, you're bound to find some that work. Here, licorice and pear do the trick. Green apple-flavored candies from the supermarket add to the theme.

KING JACK

The undisputed king of Halloween has got to be the not-so-lowly pumpkin. Each year, we transform this hapless squash into a multitude of spooky, jolly smiles that could rival DaVinci's Mona Lisa. Inspired by the vintage Halloween cover from the "Saturday Evening Post" (bottom left), our King Jack decor is full of the warm colors of the autumn season.

THE SATURDAY EVENING POST
An Ill... ly
Founded A... ...ly Franklin
OCTOBER 28, 1922   5¢ THE COPY

ELIZABETH ALEXANDER - HUGH MACNAIR KAHLER - DOROTHY DeJAGERS
L. B. YATES - WALTER De LEON - GRACE LOVELL BRYAN - GEORGE WESTON

Gilded Pumpkin, Crown, and Candle Stand

Up to this point, you have learned how to transform those cheap plastic trick-or-treat pumpkin buckets into silvery masterpieces and green goblins. Now, it's time to go for the gold—gilded gold, that is!

MATERIALS

- Plastic pumpkin
- 3 Delta Gilding Kits
- 36"-tall wooden candlestick
- 1 sheet heavy poster board
- Several artificial autumn pumpkins, leaves, and berry sprays
- 1 can Design Masters gold spray paint
- Masking tape
- 6 yards* decorative gimp trim
- Crown pattern (page 112)
- Hot glue gun and glue sticks
- Measuring tape
- Scissors
- Earthquake putty (optional)

*This yardage may vary depending on the size of the pumpkin you use and, therefore, the size of the crown that is made. Our plastic pumpkin was quite large by comparison to most of those found in stores.

For the head and crown:

1. Spray paint the pumpkin gold and allow it to dry.

2. Gild the plastic pumpkin according to product instructions on the kit. Set aside.

3. Measure around top of pumpkin to determine the size of the crown needed to fit.

4. Using the pattern on page 112, trace the tall crown onto the poster board, making sure the base of the crown motif is repeated enough times to accomplish the length you obtained from measuring in step 3.

5. Cut crown pattern out.

6. Hot glue the gimp around all edges of crown and spray paint crown gold.

7. Use more gilding on the crown.

8. Tape crown closed on the backside and cover masking tape with the gold spray paint.

9. Hot glue a small autumn pumpkin onto each crown point.

10. Hot glue crown to pumpkin head.

11. Wire and hot glue the rest of the autumn berries, pumpkins, and leaves into a lively arrangement, and using a piece of the wire from the stems, hook this arrangement to the front of the crown.

For the candle stand:

1. Spray paint and gild the candlestick as in steps 1 and 2 of the previous instructions above.

2. Set King Jack on top, using the spike (found on all those large candlesticks) to steady him. If needed, add a little earthquake putty under him to secure in place.

The True King Jack

The real King Jack was actually a man named John Czeszeziczski, which was later changed to just "Cz" for obvious reasons. In the early 1930s, Cz had the idea of growing the face right on the pumpkin as opposed to simply carving it. He set about (on his farm in Madison, Ohio) fashioning molds from crockery, glass, and iron, but all cracked under the strain of the growing orange orbs. Finally, he lit upon the idea of using aluminum. It worked. He began fashioning masks that bolted to the still green pumpkin in the shape of skulls, himself, his wife, and movie stars of the era such as Clark Gable and then-President Franklin D. Roosevelt. Cz became famous in his area and his pumpkins sold from $10 to $50—an unheard-of sum in Depression Era America. It's unclear what ever became of Cz and his "head-making hobby," but many years later, people digging around what once was his farm were very surprised to unearth these long-forgotten aluminum faces. Today, the molds in good condition sell for more than a $1,000.

Gilded Pumpkin
Place Card Holders

These tiny pumpkins are merely a miniature variation of our grand King Jack. Not only do they help maintain the continuity of the entire King Jack theme on your table, but they also serve the practical purpose of letting your guests know where they are to sit.

1. Spray paint the six small plastic pumpkins gold and allow them to dry.

2. Gild each plastic pumpkin according to product instructions on the kit. Set aside.

3. Wire together the autumn berries, leaves, and tiny pumpkins into artful little arrangements that match that of your King Jack display, as shown below.

4. Place each arrangement inside each small pumpkin.

5. Cut out enough bats (one for each person) from the cardstock, using the pattern on page 112.

6. Use gold paint pen to write a name on each bat cutout, and fold, as shown below.

7. Tuck bat into small pumpkin arrangement so name is clearly visible.

Festive Fiesta Ware

The incredible pumpkin plate chargers, mugs, and matching candlesticks shown on the table above are by Fiesta Ware. The "chargers" are actually called pizza plates and all can be found on Fiesta Ware's Web site (see Resources, page 127). Nothing will make your Halloween more perfect year after year than to have this unusual, handsome dinnerware added to your table.

Make extra small arrangements to match the ones on the pumpkin crown and place cards. Set them about to glitter in the light as shown above.

The House That Jack Built

IN A KINGDOM FAR, FAR AWAY, NEAR THE BEND IN THE WILD, WILD RIVER,
LIES THE COUNTRY ESTATE OF OUR GOOD FRIEND JACK. IF YOU EVER
WONDERED WHO TRULY GREW ALL THE MAGICAL PUMPKINS FOR
HALLOWEEN NIGHT, NOW YOU KNOW. AND YOU ALSO KNOW WHERE IT ALL
HAPPENS! TO REPLICATE THIS DARLING DOMICILE FOR USE AS A CENTERPIECE
ON A DINNER TABLE OR AS DECORATION SOMEWHERE ELSE IN YOUR HOME,
ALL YOU NEED ARE SOME MINIATURE DOLLHOUSE PARTS, A RATHER LARGE
PUMPKIN, AND WHITE SPRAY PAINT.

MATERIALS

- Large pumpkin
  (or artificial Fun-Kin style)
- 1 dollhouse doorway
  by Roses Doll House
- 2 dollhouse windows
  by Roses Doll House
- 4 picket fence sections
  by Roses Doll House
- 1 can white spray paint
- 1 package quilt pins
- Fine-tip black marking pen
- Masking tape
- Hot glue gun and glue sticks
- Carving knife
- Artificial grass or moss
  (optional)
- Fresh broccoli (optional)
- 1 bunch baby's breath
  (optional)
- 6" figural man (optional)

1. Cover any "glass" in the windows and doors with masking tape.

2. Paint all windows, doors, and fence pieces with several coats of white spray paint. Allow them to dry in between coats.

3. Hollow out pumpkin from top as you would normally for a jack-o-lantern.

4. Lay the doorframe on the nicest and flattest side of the pumpkin.

5. Stick a quilt pin into the pumpkin at all four corners of the inside frame and take away the doorframe.

6. Use the marking pen to "connect the dots" or in this case the pins, creating a rectangular front door opening.

7. Follow the marked rectangle as you cut the door opening.

8. Insert door into opening. Cut away a little more pumpkin inside the opening, if needed.

9. Repeat steps 4 through 8 for the windows.

10. Place fence sections as desired and hold them together with a touch of hot glue to form right angles.

11. Arrange the fence and embellish the "yard" as desired with such items as artificial grass, a figural "Jack," or broccoli and baby's breath, which make excellent shrubs and flower bushes.

Here's Jack, gathering some of his wildflowers out of the garden to grace his Halloween night table.

*This is the farmer,
sowing the corn,
That kept the cock
that crowed in the morn,
That waked the priest
all shaven and shorn,
That married the man
all tattered and torn,
That kissed the maiden
all forlorn,
That milked the cow
with the crumpled horn,
That tossed the dog,
That worried the cat,
That killed the rat,
That ate the malt,
That lay in the house
that Jack built.*

—The Real Mother Goose
1916 Rand McNally & Co.

Haunted HINT

Keep in mind that dollhouse-building accessories are usually done 1" to 1-foot scale, so your doorway and door jam could easily be 8" or 9" tall. You're going to need one big pumpkin!

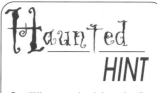
There stands Jack, all dressed up for the evening's festivities. His house is ready to receive the guests that will soon be arriving.

As night falls Jack stands at his door ready to greet his guests as they arrive. The fire is lit inside and the buffet table has been readied with all sorts of delectable treats befitting a resident of the fairy kingdom he presides over.

With the party over, Jack bids a sad adieu to his party friends, knowing full-well that on the morrow, he must rise to start the plans for next year's gala event.

CANDIES AND CANDLES

Want an easy yet perfectly fitting theme for decorating a Halloween party? This next little section can be made as jovial as you want using mostly Halloween candies that come in orange and black and adding in the column candles to match gives it just a hint of sophistication.

Column Candleholders in Black

GATHER AND COLLECT A HOST OF COLUMN CANDLEHOLDERS FROM TAG SALES AND INEXPENSIVE STORES AND YOU WILL SOON HAVE THE MAKINGS FOR CANDLE ACCENTS TO GLOW AROUND YOUR HOME.

Haunted HINT

Although this project is incredibly simple, you can see from the photo that the finished project looks quite nice. The key to adding an extra bit of flair is in choosing some not-so-ordinary candles. Ours in the orange and black candy-stripe motif help dress up our entire affair.

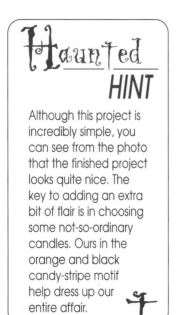

MATERIALS

- Several column-style candleholders in different sizes
- 1 can Design Masters Glossy Black Spray Paint
- 1 orange, black, or white column candle for each holder
- Newspaper

1. Place column candleholders on newspaper in a well-ventilated room or outside.

2. Spray paint with glossy black paint and let dry.

3. Repeat with a second coat of paint, if necessary.

4. Add candles to the tops and place decoratively on your table.

Dishtowel Table Runner

MATERIALS

- 4 matching woven 18" x 24" Halloween dishtowels
- 11 yards woven gimp trim
- 2 matching 4" tassels
- 3 yards complimentary Halloween fabric
- Matching thread
- Scissors or rotary cutter
- Straight pins
- Sewing machine
- Iron
- Yardstick

WITH ALL THE GREAT HALLOWEEN DISHTOWELS OUT THERE, WHY NOT BUY A FEW TO USE AS DECOR? SEWN END TO END AND LINED WITH A COORDINATING FABRIC, THESE OTHERWISE DEMURE TOWELS CAN BE CREATIVELY CONVERTED AND USED AS RUNNERS, PLACEMATS, OR NAPKINS.

1. Carefully cut through the thread seams where the towels have been hemmed and press hems open flat.

2. With ½" seam allowance, stitch towels end to end.

3. Using the sewn-together dishtowels as a template, cut a length of fabric to be used as lining.

4. Pin together with right sides facing.

5. To trim ends into points, fold runner down the center lengthwise. Then, using a yardstick as a straight edge guide, cut 8" off each end at an angle.

6. To attach the lining, begin ½" from the outer edge of the pinned pieces, stitch all the way around outer edges, leaving a small opening for turning near center.

7. Clip points, turn right-side out, and press flat.

8. Topstitch gimp trim around entire perimeter of runner, being sure to close up the turn-hole opening as you go.

9. Handstitch one tassel to each end.

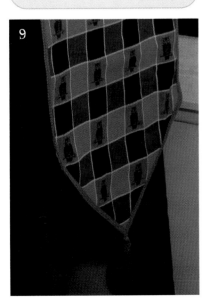

9

Lace Cake Stand Toppers

HERE'S A WONDERFUL AND QUICK DECORATIVE
TOUCH: COVER A PEDESTAL CAKE STAND WITH ITS
OWN TOPPER SIMPLY DRIPPING IN LACE.

MATERIALS

- Pedestal cake stand
- ½-yard 36"-wide orange or black felt
- 2½ yards heavy white lace
- 1 package Rit dye to match felt
- White chalk
- Straight pins
- White thread
- Scissors or rotary cutter
- Sewing machine
- Iron

1. Dye lace according to Rit package instructions for the stovetop method. (Rit dye makes a lot of dye bath, so if you want anything else dyed, now's the time.)

2. Using the top of the cake stand as a template, turn the stand upside-down onto the felt and use the chalk to draw a line around it.

3. Add ½" all the way around and cut out.

4. Use the first felt piece as a guide for cutting the second piece the same size.

5. With right sides of lace and one felt circle together (decorative lace edge pointing to center of circle), evenly gather lace around edge of felt, pin to hold, and stitch in place using ¼" seam allowance.

6. Carefully keeping all lace sandwiched to the inside, add second felt circle on top of the other and pin together.

7. Stitch around circumference ½" from edge, leaving a small opening for turning.

8. Turn right-side out and lightly press felt.

9. Topstitch in ½" from edge, being sure to close up turn-hole at the same time. Felt should lay flat.

Always use a plate between any cake and your lace topper, as shown above.

Did You Know?

If you thought a lighted candle in a fresh, damp pumpkin was just about as dangerous as one can get, think again. The book "Games For Hallowe'en," published in 1912, actually suggested its readers make a ghoulish face out of a cardboard box, cover the eyes and mouth with colored tissue paper, and place the box over the lit gas jets in the parlor. Now that's scary!

Black-and-orange honeycomb tissue paper balls have been around for a long time. Ours came from the Beistle Company (Resources, page 127), which has been making Halloween and other holiday paper decorations for more than a century.

Paper Lanterns

PAPER LANTERNS, EVEN IF NOT LIT UP, MAKE ANY ROOM FESTIVE. THE JACK-O-LANTERN AND SMALL SKULL MOTIFS SHOWN IN THE PROJECT PHOTO CAME READY TO LIGHT. FOR THE POLKA-DOTTED ONES, THOUGH, YOU HAVE TO GET CRAFTING!

MATERIALS

- Several sizes white paper lanterns (available at Cost Plus Stores)
- 1 package orange dot stickers
- 1 can Design Masters Glossy Black Spray Paint
- Newspaper

1. Remove five to six sheets of orange dots from their packaging. (Exact number of sheets depends on the size of your paper lanterns.)

2. Spread out on newspaper and spray with the black spray paint.

3. When dry, peel and stick the dots to the opened paper lanterns, alternating in a random pattern with the orange dots.

4. Hang the finished lanterns.

Paper Party Hats with Clip Art Owls and Bats

LET'S CONTINUE WITH THE POLKA-DOT THEME FOR
SOME OLD-FASHIONED PARTY HATS. THESE ARE
EASY TO MAKE AND ARE A GREAT WAY TO ADD AN
EXTRA DASH OF FRIVOLITY TO YOUR PARTY.

Detail of candles and candies above.

MATERIALS

- 6 black conical party hats
- 1 roll orange crepe paper streamer
- 1 roll black crepe paper streamer
- 1 package orange dot stickers
- 3 sheets orange cardstock (8½" x 11")
- Scissors
- Owl and bat clip art (page 118)
- Black thread
- Sewing machine
- Hot glue gun and glue sticks
- Yardstick
- Copy machine, or home computer, scanner, and printer

1. Using the clip art on page 118, have these images printed in black on orange cardstock at your local copy center, or if you prefer, scan them into your own computer and print them out yourself. One image for each hat.

2. Peel and stick the orange dots onto the black cone hats, as shown at left.

3. For ruffle, cut 2 yards each of the black and orange crepe paper streamers.

4. Lay one streamer piece on top of the other and machine stitch down their centers, bunching into pleats as you go.

5. Carefully separate the orange from the black along the edges. Use a gentle hand as the crepe paper is easy to tear.

6. Hot glue the ruffle of crepe paper to the bottom of the hat.

7. Top hat with a clip art critter attached with more hot glue.

Haunted HINT

While you're at it, use some other incredible vintage clip art images and have them printed onto an 8½" x 11" piece of orange cardstock. Spray paint an old oval frame black with Design Masters spray paint and frame the clip art piece for a truly good-looking decoration, as shown in the photo at right. Embellish the set-up with orange candy canes. Yes, we said orange. We found the ones shown here last Christmas for just such a purpose.

THE HAUNTED HOUSEHOLD

The treats in this section aren't nearly as tricky as their finished elegance makes them appear. They provide just the right decorative touches to add some Halloween flair to any space, whether a guest bedroom, front door, or outdoor walkway.

A Jolly Halloween

Trixie LeTreat Character Wreath®

THE PERFECT HALLOWEEN WITCH (AND COVER GIRL OF THIS BOOK),
TRIXIE LETREAT IS READY TO DISH OUT THE GOODIES ON HALLOWEEN
NIGHT. FOR ALL HER MATERIALS, STEPS, AND "BEAUTY," AND ALTHOUGH
COMPLETING HER IS NOT AS SIMPLE AS IT WOULD BE IF SAMANTHA WERE
HERE TO MERELY TWITCH HER NOSE, MADAME TRIXIE IS ACTUALLY QUITE
EASY TO MAKE—ESPECIALLY IF YOU HAVE DIAN AT DBD ENTERPRISES PAINT
HER FACE AS WE DID. WITCH'S HONOR!

MATERIALS

- 14" straw wreath
- Small handsaw
- Packing tape
- 6 2" nails
- 1 yard 36"-wide black felt
- ½-yard 45"-wide black chiffon fabric
- Hand-painted porcelain doll head #DB520 from DBD
- 1 package curly lambs wool
- 1 ornate black button
- 8" cardboard cake circle
- 10" square scrap heavy cardboard
- 3 yards pregathered black lace
- 1 can DAPtex Insulating Foam Sealant
- Emery board
- 3 wooden gingerbread men cutouts
- 3 2" wooden disks
- 1 package lollipop sticks (or wooden craft sticks)
- 1 box plaster of Paris

- Delta Ceramcoat Acrylic Paint
  - 2-oz. bottle orange
  - 2-oz. bottle chocolate brown
  - 2-oz. bottle black
- 12 small brown pleated cupcake and candy papers in two sizes (6 each size)
- Wilton candy mold, any variety
- 10 various tiny Halloween buttons and cake decorations
- 1 can clear sealant
- 1 tube Creative Beginnings Ultra Fine Gold Diamond Dust Glitter
- Black paint pen
- Orange paint pen
- Top from an old spray can (spray paint, hairspray, etc.)
- Hot glue gun and glue sticks
- Witch hat and sleeve patterns (pages 110, 111, and 114)

WITCH TRIVIA

In Italy, at Christmastime a friendly witch named La Befana distributes toys and goodies to children.

For the head:

1. With hot glue gun, add curly lambs wool to porcelain doll head and tie it up in a bun, bringing a few tendrils down the left side. Set head aside.

2. Using the hat pattern on page 111, cut one cone shape of black felt and two circle brim pieces.

3. With the pattern on page 110, cut one circle brim piece from 10" cardboard scrap.

4. Using a ¼" seam allowance, stitch the two felt brim pieces together around outer edge.

5. Trim felt close to stitch line, turn right-side out, and press.

6. Slip cardboard between felt pieces, trimming it a little if needed. Use a denim or upholstery needle to machine stitch around inner perimeter of brim. Set brim piece aside.

7. Stitch cone edges together, trim, and turn right-side out.

8. Whipstitch cone to underside of brim.

9. Cut a 4½ " by 45" strip from the black chiffon.

10. Fold lengthwise and using a ½" seam allowance, machine stitch together, leaving a small turn-hole opening.

11. Turn stitched chiffon strip and press.

12. Wrap chiffon strip around base of hat two or three times and tie in a knot in back, leaving both ends hanging down about 10".

13. Hot glue hat to head and set all aside.

For the sleeves:

1. Cut two 9½" x 12" rectangles from black felt. These are the Lower Sleeves.

2. Cut one 7" x 9½" rectangle from black felt. This will be the Neck Area.

3. Using pattern, page 114, cut two Upper Sleeves from black felt.

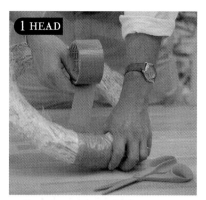

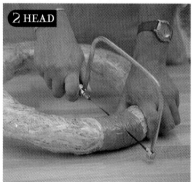

4. With ½" seam allowance, stitch Upper Sleeve pieces together at points indicated on pattern to form pleats.

5. Using the illustration at right for guidance, gather bottom of Upper Sleeve in to fit the 9½" side of Lower Sleeve rectangle. Stitch Upper Sleeve to Lower Sleeve. Repeat for other side.

6. Gather the top of Upper Sleeve in to fit the 9½" side of the Neck Area rectangle. Stitch Upper Sleeve to neck area. Repeat for other sleeve.

7. With right sides together, stitch along entire length of sleeves: from end of cuff, across neck area, and to other cuff.

8. Turn right-side out, being careful not to stretch the felt out of shape.

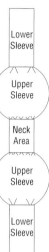

Lower Sleeve

Upper Sleeve

Neck Area

Upper Sleeve

Lower Sleeve

Assembling the head and body:

1. At any point on wreath, circle with about a 3" area of packing tape, as shown at left.

2. Carefully saw through wreath at center of taped area and tape off raw wreath ends so straw will not "leak" out, as shown in the progression of photos at left.

3. Slip finished sleeve onto wreath.

4. Affix head to wreath using hot glue on the back of the porcelain neck area.

5. Push the 2" nails through the holes in the headpiece for extra sturdiness.

6. Wrap the rest of the black chiffon from the hat around neck and wreath in a crisscross manner.

7. Handstitch the chiffon from the back of the hat under the chin and cover stitches with fancy black button. Set aside.

For the treat tray:

1. Fill the brown paper cupcake/candy wrappers with enough of the DAPtex so it rises over the top like soft serve ice cream. Allow these "treats" to dry overnight.

2. Paint the DAPtex sweets with orange paint, sprinkle with glitter while paint is still wet, and let dry.

3. Decorate each treat with a candy with a decorative button on top as well as red berries, green leaves, and little "dollops" of glittered black paint.

4. Mix the plaster of Paris according to box instructions and spoon into the chocolate molds. Try to get as little "spillover" as possible.

5. Once they are dry, pop the plaster "chocolate" out and use an emery board to smooth their edges.

6. Paint each plaster chocolate with the brown paint. Let dry.

Did You Know?
Witch trials started as early as 1275 and lasted well into the 1700s in many countries.

7. Highlight the chocolates with orange paint and dust with glitter while paint is still wet.

8. Paint gingerbread boy cutouts with two or three coats of brown paint and let dry.

9. When dry, add painted trim squeezed on from paint pens.

10. Spray with clear sealant and dust with glitter.

11. Paint wooden disks with two or three coats of orange paint. Let dry.

12. Swirl painted orange disks with black paint and let dry.

13. Spray disks with clear sealant and glitter and hot glue lollypop sticks to back.

14. Use hot glue to edge cake circle with black lace and then glue tarts and candies to it.

15. Hot glue the spray can lid to center of tray to build up a second layer of goodies.

16. Hot glue cupcake treats (about 16 of them) onto tray, hiding all of the cardboard and paint lid.

17. Hot glue gingerbread boys and lollypops in place and fill in any open spaces with red and orange berries.

18. Attach "plate of goodies" to wreath hands using a couple of 2" nails carefully poked through the cardboard and into the straw wreath. This will make it removable for future storage.

Detail of finished treat tray above. Notice how we sprinkled everything with glitter by first applying a coat of clear sealant and adding the glitter while still wet. As a final touch, we added a small glass jack-o-lantern ornament to the top center of the tray arrangement.

Looking as though it just blew in from the Land of Oz, the Witch's House in Beverly Hills, California (at left), was originally built in 1921 as part of a silent screen movie studio. In 1926, it was moved to its present location and is the private home of Michael Libow, who is happily restoring it. Tour busses pass many times daily.

Deadly Night Shades

WELL, MAYBE THESE SHADES ARE NOT THAT DEADLY, BUT THEY SURE HAVE A KILLER LOOK. INTERCHANGE THEM WITH ANY OF YOUR EXISTING LAMPSHADES, AND YOU WILL CREATE THE AMBIANCE OF HALLOWEEN IN ANY ROOM WITHOUT MUCH TROUBLE AT ALL.

MATERIALS

- 1 package holiday printed tissue
- 1 small Peel and Stick Hollywood Lights Lampshade
- 1 package clear glass glitter beads without holes
- White glue
- Scissors
- Newspaper
- 2" paintbrush
- Hot glue gun and glue sticks
- Pre-strung black beads*
- Black gimp trim*

*The yardage amount for these depends on the size of lampshade chosen and can usually be found printed on the label of the lampshade.

1. Spread out and smooth one sheet of the tissue on a tabletop.

2. Peel away the protective paper layer from the lampshade.

3. Do not use the paper backing as a pattern as instructed on the lampshade. Unlike fabric, you are using delicate tissue paper and it will adhere instantly with no going back.

4. Carefully place the lampshade down on the center of the tissue and roll it very slowly to avoid wrinkling.

5. Trim away all excess paper.

6. Spread a piece of newspaper to work over and in small areas at a time, use the paintbrush to coat the lampshade with a clear-drying white glue (such as Elmer's).

7. Sprinkle on the glass beads until lampshade is completely covered and let dry.

8. Once dry, hot glue the bead trim around the bottom.

9. Hot glue the decorative gimp on top of bead trim and around top edge of lampshade.

Halloween Bed Sheets

Materials

- Set all-cotton white bed sheets
- Vintage cat (page 119) or other Halloween clip art
- Scissors
- 11" x 17" sheet paper
- Color copier, or home computer, scanner, and color printer
- Iron
- Transfer paper (optional)

ȘCARED AT NIGHT? ȚUST HIDE UNDER THESE SHEETS. HERE'S A TROUBLE-FREE PROJECT THAT'LL KEEP YOU IN THAT HOLIDAY FRAME OF MIND EVEN WHEN BEING TUCKED IN AT NIGHT.

1. Wash and dry sheets.

2. Have your piece of Halloween artwork reduced to a more manageable size on a color copier at your local copy center. Or, if you prefer, scan the images into your own home computer and manipulate the sizing yourself.

3. Now make as many copies of the single image as you can fit onto a sheet of 11" x 17" paper.

4. Cut them out and paste them onto a blank sheet of 11" x 17" paper. Or, if you are using your own computer, simply copy and paste the images again and again onto an 11" x 17" document.

5. Then, either take your paste-up 11" x 17" to your local copy center and have the images put onto transfer paper for fabrics, or simply print the document on your computer directly to transfer paper that can be put through your color printer.

6. Cut out each image and arrange them along the top edge of the top sheet and side edges of each pillowcase.

7. Use a hot iron to press them into place.

At left, detail of pillowcase cat placement.

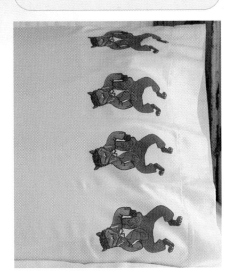

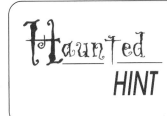

Haunted HINT

In step 2, remember to put your image on the top sheet upside-down to the hemmed top edge so that when you make the bed and turn the sheet down over the top of your blankets, the image will be right-side up. Also, Kinko's Copy Stores charge by the press, so you will want to do as many at one time as you can. Even if these start adding up, you'll have a wonderful, vintage-looking scareloom that you will treasure for years.

Vintage Puddy-Tat Pillows

While you're making decorative sheets and pillowcases, why not have more vintage artwork transferred onto plain muslin for small decorative throw pillows? We chose all black cats for our theme, but any spooky Halloween theme would work.

MATERIALS

- 1 yard muslin
  (yields several small pillows)
- 1 yard 45"-wide backing
  fabric (any color/print)
- 3 yards ¼" cotton cording
- Batting for filler
- Scissors or rotary cutter
- Hand-sewing needle
- Thread
- Sewing machine
- Zipper foot
- Iron
- Color copier, or
  home computer, scanner,
  and color printer
- Vintage Halloween artwork
  (pages 120-121)
- Transfer paper (optional)

Pillow detail shown above.

Preparing the pillow pieces:

1. Wash and dry all muslin before having anything printed on it.

2. Once you have determined the size of your pillow, place the clip art design where desired and cut square or rectangle around it, including suitable ½" seam allowance all the way around. Our largest pillow only measured 7" x 9" finished.

3. Then take the clip art and muslin pillow front to your local copy center and have the image transferred to the muslin. Or, you may scan the image into your own computer, print it out on transfer paper that is suitable for fabric, and iron it into place on the muslin pillow front.

4. Using the front muslin piece as a template, cut a suitable backing fabric the same size to match.

5. To make the self-welting around the pillows edges, cut 3"-wide strips of the backing fabric on the bias.

6. Using ½" seam allowance, sew strips end to end and press seams open flat.

7. Sandwich the cotton cording into the middle of the strip, and using the zipper foot attachment on your sewing machine, stitch the fabric closed right up to the cording. This will leave a bit of a lip to sew it into the pillow.

Putting pillow together:

1. Starting at the center bottom of the muslin pillow front piece and with right sides together, stitch the covered cording to the muslin front piece using the zipper foot.

2. Cut off excess cording, leaving about 2" free on each end. This "tail" will later be tucked up inside the pillow.

3. Place backing piece right sides together with front and use the zipper foot to sew around the perimeter of the pillow, leaving a 2" opening in the center bottom for turning and stuffing.

4. Turn pillow and press if needed.

5. Stuff tight with batting.

6. Tuck cording ends up inside of pillow and use small hand stitches to whipstitch pillow closed.

Old-Time Felt Pillows and Throw

RESTING ON AN ANTIQUE BED ONCE OWNED BY
ROBERT TODD LINCOLN (ABE'S SON), THESE BRAND-
NEW FELT GOODIES HAVE A TRUE VINTAGE FEEL
THANKS TO THE OLD GRAPHICS USED ON THEM.

MATERIALS (PILLOW AND THROW COMBINED)

- ½-yard 36"-wide black felt
- ¾-yard 36"-wide orange felt
- ½-yard 36"-wide white felt
- 4 yards 72"-wide black felt
- 2¼ yards 72"-wide orange felt
- 1 yard 72"-wide white felt
- ½-yard Heavy Duty Heat 'n Bond
- 1 spool each orange and black thread
- 16-oz. bag Fiber-fill
- Straight pins
- Sewing machine

- Scissors or rotary cutter
- Vintage Halloween art (pages 122-126) or 1 package new Beistle cutout decorations
- 2 skeins black yarn
- #16 5cm steel yarn needle (or similar large-eye needle with sharper point for felt)
- Iron
- Color copier, or home computer, scanner, and color printer

Beginning the pillow:

1. Cut black felt into two 18" squares. These will be the front and back of the pillow.

2. Cut eight 4½" x 36" strips from the orange felt.

3. With right sides facing, center one orange strip on one edge of one black felt square and pin in place. Be sure the strip is centered and the ends extend way beyond the edges of the square.

4. With ½" seam allowance, stitch strip to felt square, as shown below.

5. Repeat steps 3 and 4 for remaining sides on both black felt squares.

6. Once you have attached the edge strips to all four sides of the pillow, press all seams inward toward center square, as shown (6A), clipping the corners as needed (6B) so all will lay flat.

7. Fold top strip at right angel *over* bottom strip, press, and pin, as shown (7A and 7B).

8. Trim excess "tails" away from both strips, as shown below.

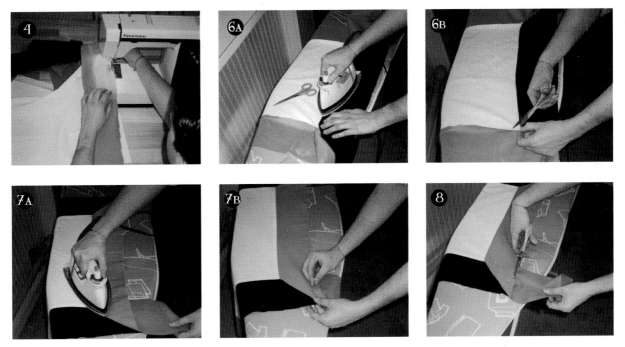

Note: The fabrics shown here in the how-to photos are for illustrative purposes only and do not match the actual fabrics used for this project.

9. Using matching thread, topstitch mitered corner very close to edge, as shown at left. Be sure to use a backstitch at the beginning so thread won't pull out.

10. Repeat steps 8 and 9 for other corners.

11. Press and cut away excess material under both the pillow front and back pieces.

12. With matching orange thread and from the underneath side, topstitch the inner seam flat to orange banding.

Assembling the pillow:

1. Lay front and back of pillow right sides together and pin at inner black felt square.

2. Match mitered orange felt corners and pin.

3. Stitch along outside orange banding starting near (but never on) one corner. Use a full 1" seam allowance to give orange banding added sturdiness. Be sure to leave a 3" opening for turning and stuffing.

4. Clip all corners and remove pins.

5. Turn pillow right-side out, being careful not to stretch the felt out of shape. Lightly press.

6. Re-pin black felt at corners and use black thread to topstitch ½" into the black, *starting at the same point as the opening left in the orange felt.*

7. Topstitch ½" into the orange banding using orange thread. Set aside.

Adding the pillow image:

1. Reduce or enlarge Halloween clip art to fit your pillow front either by taking it to your local copy center or doing it yourself by scanning it into your home computer.

2. Transfer the image onto fabric transfer paper. Again, this step can be done either at the copy center, or you can print the image from your computer directly onto transfer paper placed within your color printer.

3. Using a hot iron, press the image onto piece of white felt large enough to accommodate your image.

4. Press white felt image onto Heat 'n Bond, according to instructions.

5. Cut out image.

6. Again referring to the package instructions, press the bonded felt image onto felt pillow front.

Finishing the pillow:

1. Stuff pillow (but not banding) with Fiber-fill.

2. Close opening by machine stitching in both black and orange areas. Be sure to use matching thread in each of the different-colored areas.

3. Close original opening in orange felt banding by blanket stitching (instructions next page) with the black yarn around entire perimeter of orange banding.

Did You Know? The Beistle Co. of Pennsylvania, which was founded in 1900 by Martin Luther Beistle, is one of today's largest holiday paper product producers. Many of its embossed cardboard Halloween designs from yesteryear command high prices now. All the die-cuts in this project are vintage Beistle from the '50s and '60s. If you want to hunt down these treasured paper goods, another name to look for is H.E. Luhrs, Beistle's son-in-law who later became company president.

For blanket stitch:

1. Starting at left corner with about 18" of black yarn and a #16 needle, insert needle from back side to emerge at tip of corner, leaving 1" to 2" of thread hidden between the fabrics. Do not knot thread and do not pull thread through.

2. From corner, over ½" and down ½", insert the needle in front only through the first layer of felt. Refer to diagram at right.

3. While holding hidden thread between left index finger and thumb, pull most of yarn through, leaving some slack at top.

4. From back, pass needle under yarn toward front, then up, so you emerge at edge of fabric directly above first hole.

5. Pick up yarn with needle, back through front, and pull it taut across the top ½".

5. Continue in same manner (steps 2 through 5). You may wish to hold each stitch with your left index finger and thumb until the next stitch is completed.

6. To turn corners, place three stitches in same hole, as shown in the diagram.

7. At end of each 18" length of yarn, simply thread yarn between fabrics 2" or 3" and cut off.

BLANKET STITCHING

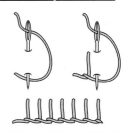

Detail of throw's mitered corner.

Those great old paper pulp pumpkins shown on the felt throw (project photo, page 84) and above are actually brand-new. Made by a company called Season's Gone By (Resources, page 128), these new ones sell for considerably less than the original ones do. They also come with the original tissue paper insert of goofy eyes and scary grins. But don't light these pumpkins with a candle as many people did with the originals. (Now you know why finding an original is so costly!)

For the felt throw:

These instructions are almost identical to that of the pillow. Exceptions: the orange banding only appears on the throw front and it is not stuffed.

1. Cut a 60" square of black felt, setting the rest of the black felt aside for later use.

2. Cut four 6" x 81"-wide strips from the orange felt and stitch to black square as in the steps 3 through 5 of the "Beginning the pillow"instructions, page 85.

3. Miter the corners of the orange banding according to the instructions given in steps 6 through 9 in the "Beginning the pillow"instructions.

4. With right sides facing, lay the banded piece on top of the remaining black felt. Pin around perimeter of orange banding and trim away any excess black felt on the lining piece.

5. Using ½" seam allowance, stitch, leaving a 10" turn-opening (never at a corner).

6. Clip corners, turn, and lightly press.

7. Add vintage designs according to steps 1 through 6 in the "Adding the pillow image" instructions on previous page.

8. Use black yarn to edge around entire throw according to the instructions under "Blanket stitching the pillow" above.

Baby Imps

DANCING ALL AROUND THE PLACE WITH THEIR BRIGHT
RED NAKED BEHINDS, THESE LITTLE IMPS WILL STEAL
YOUR HEART SINCE THEY COST VERY LITTLE TO MAKE
AND YOU CAN SET THEM JUST ABOUT ANYWHERE.

MATERIALS

- 3 small all-vinyl baby dolls
- 1 can Design Masters Holiday Red Spray Paint
- 1 package Fimo Modeling Compound (any color)
- Sharpie black pen
- 3 white pumpkins (any size)
- Several red pomegranates
- 3 black sponge bats*
- Masking tape
- Staple gun
- Scissors
- Hot glue gun and glue sticks

*These bats can be found in craft stores, such as Michael's.

1. Form three sets of tiny horns from the Fimo and bake according to package instructions.

2. Hot glue horns to the little baby dolls' foreheads.

3. Cover eyes with masking tape and spray paint each doll completely red.

4. Cut the head from each sponge bat and staple the remaining wing pieces to center backs of red imps.

5. Draw in little arched eyebrows on the face with the Sharpie.

6. To display, stack pumpkins and apples on a table and add those cute little devils.

Close-up of a Baby Imp. For a pretty arrangement, try setting him on a white pumpkin in a bowl filled with red apples and pepper berries.

Mark isn't sure what to make of these Baby Imps, considering Kasey made them all.

The watercolor prints shown in the three photos at left are the work of Lewis Barrett Lehrman of the Haunted Studio. They are a wonderful addition to any Halloween setting, but they're so gorgeous that we leave them up year-round. For more information, see Resources, page 127. Can you find the hidden spooks in the paintings?

A Jolly Halloween

Little Girl Witch Doll

BASED ON AN ANTIQUE POSTCARD AND THE FACT
THAT THESE DOLLS BY DAISY KINGDOM LOOKED AN
AWFUL LIKE HER, THIS PROJECT SEEMED A NATURAL
TO CREATE.

MATERIALS

- 15" "Pansy Doll" #4034-12110 by Daisy Kingdom
- 1 yard 45" white border eyelet fabric
- 1¼ yard ⅜" red ribbon
- ¼-yard 36"-wide red felt
- 1 yard 45"-wide red satin
- 12" square scrap poster board
- 8" square scrap cardboard
- 1 yard black gimp trim
- 3M Spray Mount Adhesive
- Denim-weight needle for sewing machine
- Sewing machine
- 1 package white Velcro® dots
- Scissors
- Straight pins
- Iron
- Hat and dress patterns (pages 110, 111, and 113)

For the hat:

1. Cut brim and cone of hat from cardboard using the patterns, pages 110-111.

2. Cut out two matching circles from red felt and two from satin to fit brim.

3. Cut matching cone pieces from felt and satin.

4. Spray-mount red felt to all cardboard hat pieces. Trim away excess felt around outer and inner brim circle.

5. With right sides together, machine stitch brim pieces together with ½" seam allowance.

6. Turn brim pieces right-side out and press.

7. Slip onto felt-covered cardboard brim. Set aside.

8. Whipstitch felt cone closed.

9. With right sides together, machine stitch satin cone into shape.

10. Turn right-side out and slip satin cone over felt-covered cone.

11. Trim cone base and brim center to fit doll head.

12. Exchange regular machine needle for denim needle and stitch through all layers at bottom of cone ¼" from edge. Also stitch through all layers of inner circle of brim.

13. Hot glue cone base to inner circle of brim.

14. Hot glue gimp to base of cone on hat to hide seam where cone joins brim, as shown front and back in photos above right.

15. Hot glue gimp to outside edge of brim.

16. Use tiny stitches to hold gimp down on top and bottom all the way around brim.

For the cape:

1. Cut two 19" circles by folding remaining satin in half, right sides together, and tracing around 19"-diameter tray or platter.

2. Pin together and stitch around circle ½" from edge.

3. Remove pins and trim to ¼" around stitch line.

4. Fold cape into fourths and clip a hole just large enough for scissors to fit at the point.

5. Unfold once so cape is still folded in half and cut a straight line through both layers from center hole to edge, following the fold line.

6. Enlarge hole as necessary to fit doll's neck.

7. With ½" seam allowance, stitch each cut side together up to neck hole.

8. Clip points and edges, turn right-side out, and press cape flat.

9. With ¼" seam allowance, topstitch neck hole closed.

10. Topstitch a 20" piece of red ribbon around neck hole to tie cape to doll.

For the dress:

1. Cut four bodice pieces on fold of white eyelet, using the pattern on page 113. (Do not use the border of the eyelet.)

2. Slice two of the bodice pieces up the center for the back of the bodice.

3. Stitch darts into all pieces where indicated.

4. Using ¼" seam allowance, stitch sides and shoulder seams. Press all seams open flat.

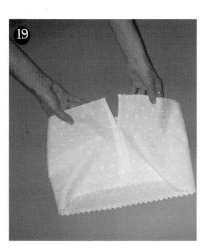

5. With right sides of bodice pieces together, stitch up back center and around neckline. Turn right-side out and press. Set aside.

6. Cut two sleeves on fold, with bottom of sleeve on eyelet border.

7. Cut two 3½" pieces of elastic.

8. Pin ends of elastic at each end of pin line on sleeve.

9. Insert machine needle into one end of elastic and sleeve material. Pull the other end of elastic and sleeve material toward you until elastic is taut. Machine stitch, holding all taut.

10. When stitched, remove from machine and sleeve bottom will be gathered.

11. Repeat steps 8 through 10 for other sleeve.

12. At top of sleeve, hand-gather ¼" from edge from one side to the other. Draw up to fit sleeve opening.

13. With right sides facing, pin middle top of sleeve to middle of sleeve opening.

14. Pin rest of sleeve in place and stitch.

15. Repeat steps 12 through 14 for other sleeve.

16. With bodice and sleeve inside out, stitch underarm of sleeve closed.

17. Turn bodice right-side out and lightly press. Set aside.

18. Cut a 27" x 9" rectangle of eyelet with border running along bottom.

19. With right-sides together, stitch back of skirt together, ending 3" from top. Press seam open flat, including the unstitched part.

20. With right sides together, align back seam opening with open back of bodice and pin on both sides.

21. Hand-gather rest of skirt evenly to fit around bodice. Pin in place and stitch with ¼" seam allowance.

22. Turn dress right-side out and press lightly, if needed.

23. Dress doll and put Velcro dots onto bodice and skirt where needed to close dress.

The inspiration for our doll was this vintage postcard, which was produced in 1909 by S. Garre from a painting by an artist named Ellen H. Clapsaddle.

Did You Know?
Apparently a gentleman in 1924 named Wallace Nutting stated in error that the designs painted on the barns of German Americans were called "hex signs," devices used to ward off evil and witches. Seems he mistranslated the phrase "sechs-shtanding Stehne," which really means six-pointed star, as either "hex" or "hexe-fuss," which is German for "witch" and "cloven-hoofed."

Tiered Clay Pot Dessert Stand

Open any home decor magazine or book and you'll find cake stands. Cake stands that are crystal, cake stands that are ceramic, stacked cake stands, tiered cake stands... the list goes on and on. Let's face it, cake stands are all the rage to display just about anything that will fit on them. Here's a bit of garden-inspired autumn whimsy to put a fresh spin on all those fancy cake stands.

Materials

- 3 clay pots in graduated sizes
- 3 clay saucers in graduated sizes
- Earthquake putty or museum wax

1. Stack the saucers on the pots in a tiered set up and secure them together with little balls of the putty all around their edges.

2. At serving time, add a plethora of harvest time treats, such as powdered sugar donuts, bright red apples, and seasonal cookies.

Mottled Leaves

The mottled-looking clay pumpkins are store-bought, but these leaves are a Kasey Rogers specialty. For yet a different twist (and fully illustrated instructions) on these mottled leaves, check out page 102 in the Thanksgiving section.

MATERIALS

- 1 large package 76 Cognac Fimo Modeling Clay
- 2-oz. bottle Forest Green Delta Ceramcoat Acrylic Paint
- 1 can 11439 Alabaster Fleck Stone by Plasti-kote
- Aluminum foil
- Several real grape leaves (or other leaves with prominent veins)
- Rolling pin
- Cookie sheet
- Small pointed X-Acto knife (or pointed kitchen knife)
- Sea sponge

Haunted HINT

To use the Tiered Clay Pot Dessert Stand and Mottled Leaves projects around your home from fall to Halloween, first turn your pumpkins with the faces to the back. When Halloween arrives, turn the jack-o-lantern faces back to the front as we have in the project photo, page 93. Then, hide those scary faces again after Halloween and continue to display through Thanksgiving.

1. Line work area and cookie sheet with foil.

2. After reading the instructions on working with Fimo, tear off a 1" to 2" chunk of the clay, crumble, and knead until soft.

3. Roll to ¼" thick with rolling pin. Remember that once you use a rolling pin to craft, it should be dedicated exclusively for that purpose. Do not use for food after using it with the Fimo.

4. Press leaf, backside down, into Fimo. Roll lightly with rolling pin to further imprint veins.

5. Trim around leaf edges with X-Acto knife and remove any excess Fimo.

6. Crumple a couple of small pieces of foil onto foil-lined cookie sheet and carefully drape leaf over them, giving the leaf a more natural, fluid shape. Vary the shape of each leaf.

7. Bake (do not microwave) according to package instructions and allow to cool.

8. Sponge paint the leaf edges with the acrylic paint and allow them to dry.

9. Give a light misting to the leaf's edges with the Alabaster Fleck Stone.

Bearded Turnips

LIGHTED TURNIPS WERE THE FORERUNNERS TO THE JACK-O-LANTERN. IN THE ANCIENT DAYS OF THE DRUIDS AND CELTICS, A BONFIRE WAS LIT ON A HILL TO MARK THE END OF THE YEAR. AT THIS POINT, ALL HEARTH FIRES WOULD BE EXTINGUISHED AND LATER RELIT FROM AN EMBER OF THE BONFIRE. TO CARRY THIS BURNING COAL HOME, A TURNIP WAS HOLLOWED OUT TO KEEP FINGERS SAFE. BEING SUPERSTITIOUS, THEY BEGAN CARVING SCARY FACES IN THEIR TURNIPS TO HELP WARD OFF ANY EVIL SPIRITS THAT MAY BE LURKING ABOUT ON THE LONG, DARK WALK BACK HOME!

MATERIALS

- Turnips with beards (roots) left on
- Baling wire
- Ice cream scoop
- Apple corer
- Small knife
- Tea lights

1. Trim top of turnip flat.

2. Use knife and ice cream scoop to hollow out turnip leaving sides about a ½" thick.

3. Use knife or apple corer to cut a pair of evil-looking eyes in the turnip.

4. Add a bailing wire handle poked into each side of the turnip, as shown bottom left (for hanging) and insert a tealight.

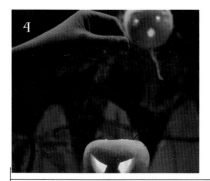

Drac's Back! Character Wreath®

HANGING IN MOCK REPOSE ONLY 12 INCHES FROM THE FINAL RESTING PLACE OF SILENT SCREEN LEGEND RUDOLPH VALENTINO, DRACULA IS AMONG GOOD COMPANY IN THE MAUSOLEUM OF THE HOLLYWOOD FOREVER MEMORIAL PARK IN HOLLYWOOD, CALIFORNIA.

1 WREATH

2 WREATH

2 WREATH

2 WREATH

MATERIALS

- 14" straw wreath
- 1 pair green knee-high nylon stockings
- Small black tuxedo jacket*
- Small formal white shirt with pleated placket and wing tip collar*
- Child-size black bow tie
- 1 yard black satin
- 1 yard red satin
- ⅓-yard heavy buckram interfacing
- 1 pair plastic vampire fangs
- 1 pair false eyelashes
- 1 pair white gloves
- 1 small costume medallion
- 2-oz. bottle Delta Ceramcoat Shiny Black Acrylic Paint

- Small amount of curly lamb's wool
- 16-oz. bag Fiber-fill
- Green eye shadow
- Small handsaw
- Packing tape
- Scissors
- Hand needle
- Green thread to match nylon stockings
- 1 package quilt pins
- Hot glue gun and glue sticks
- Fine-tipped paintbrush
- 8½" x 11" sheet tracing paper
- Several straight pins
- Patterns (page 115)

*We found our jacket and shirt at thrift stores.

Preparing the wreath:

1. Tape around about a 3½" area anywhere on the wreath, as shown.

2. Saw through center of taped area and tape the exposed edges securely, as shown in the progression of photos at left, to keep straw from falling out. Set prepared wreath aside.

For the head:

1. Tie a knot in the toe end of the stocking and clip off excess toe.

2. Stuff stocking tightly with Fiber-fill to about 8" or 9" in diameter.

3. Knot under "chin" and bring remainder of nylon stocking back down over head doubling the nylon covering it. Knot tightly again and clip excess, as shown below (3A and 3B).

4. Decide which side will be the front by looking at how the Fiber-fill "lumps" about. Pinch a nose shape, and using needle and thread, take a stitch on either side of nose. Pull thread tight so Drac's nose pops out.

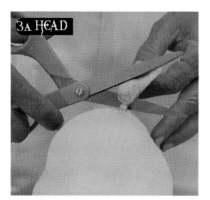

3A HEAD

3B HEAD

5. Take a stitch where the mouth would be and exit the needle well under the chin, as shown below (5A and 5B). Pull thread tight so his jaw pops a bit.

6. Clip the fangs from the rest of the fake vampire teeth and hot glue them into the jaw, as shown below.

7. Hot glue the false eyelashes in place downward, so it looks as though the eyes are shut.

8. Use a hint of green eye shadow to darken the lids in a bit.

9. Starting in the middle of the forehead, draw a black hairline into a "widow's peak" with the paint. Continue down the right side of his forehead and over to where the ears will be forming sideburns. Keep painting around base of head in back finally meeting back at the widow's peak.

10. Fill in entire top of head with black paint, making sure no green shows. Two coats were needed to make the hair sufficiently thick and shiny. Allow painted hair to dry thoroughly.

11. Add a couple of wisps of lamb's wool at the temples and to the widow's peak, as shown below.

12. Copy the ear pattern on page 115 twice onto tracing paper.

13. Pin each paper pattern to two thicknesses of nylon stocking. Leave pinned and handstitch around ear pattern line (through paper and all) leaving an opening on the side that attaches to the head.

14. Unpin and cut ears close to stitch line.

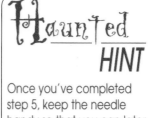

Haunted HINT

Once you've completed step 5, keep the needle handy so that you can later use it to dig deep into the nose and cheek area and pull more Fiber-fill into places you need it. Just be careful not to put a run in your stocking face!

Did You Know?
Bram Stoker's "Dracula" is the most often-filmed fictitious character. His first film appearance was in a 1920 silent film made in Russia. Unlike the infamous Count, no known print of this film survives today.

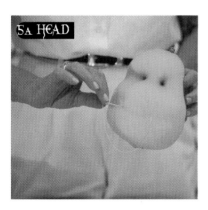

5A HEAD

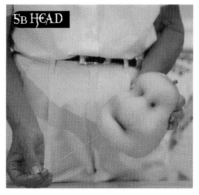

5B HEAD

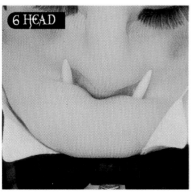

6 HEAD

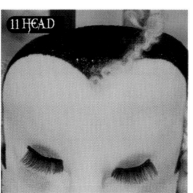

11 HEAD

15. Carefully tear all paper away along the now-perforated line and turn ear right-side out.

16. Stuff ears and whipstitch opening closed.

17. Hot glue ears to sides of head. Set head aside.

For the sleeves:
1. Cut away sleeves from tuxedo jacket.

2. Cut collar/lapel, leaving about 1" of the jacket underneath. Set aside.

3. Cut cuffs and 4" of sleeve away from the white dress shirt.

4. Cut collar with 6" of placket from shirt.

Once Drac is complete, wrap an old dead rose and a couple of its leaves with a bit of floral tape to form a boutonniere like the one pinned to the jacket in the photo above.

Lying in state? "Dracula" star, Bela Lugosi, is actually buried next to Bing Crosby in a Catholic cemetery a few miles away. Upon hearing of Lugosi's death, Jack Benny didn't miss a beat in saying, "Don't worry, he'll be back!"

5. Slip shirt cuffs onto wreath ends, leaving about 3" of wreath extending beyond them. Hold in place with hot glue and quilt pins at cut line on sleeve. Be sure the sleeves are on the proper arms.

6. Add tuxedo sleeves over shirt-sleeves so just a bit of white cuff shows.

7. Trim away any excess sleeve at top of wreath and whipstitch together the tuxedo sleeve to the shirt sleeve. The stitches need not be your best work as none of the top will show.

8. Hot glue head to top of wreath/sleeves, holding it all in place with quilt pins. Let dry.

Dress to kill:

1. Stuff the fingers only of the white gloves and slip them on the wreath ends, up under the shirt cuffs (unbutton cuffs and rebutton, if needed). The wreath will fill the palm area. Hold in place with hot glue and pins. Interlace fingers in "restful repose."

2. Unbutton placket and wrap collar around head and neck area. Rebutton and hot glue in place. If collar is too large, fold it down in back, press, and stitch before gluing in place.

3. Wrap lapel/collar around shirt collar and overlap in front. If lapels hang too long, trim from bottom, fold under, and stitch to hold. Hot glue lapel/collar at back of neck.

4. Remove banding from bow tie and hot glue in place on shirtfront.

5. Cut 36" x 45" rectangles, one each from the black and red satin.

6. With ½" seam allowance and right sides of the black and red satin rectangles together, stitch around three sides, leaving a 36" side open.

7. Clip corners, turn, and press. Set aside.

8. Using the collar pattern on page 115, cut one collar piece of red satin, one of black satin, and one of heavy buckram.

9. With ½" seam allowance and right sides of satin collar pieces facing and buckram on top, stitch around sides and top, leaving bottom open for turning.

10. Clip collar piece corners, turn, and press flat.

11. Hand-gather the open side of cape in to fit the open end of the collar. Pin with black sides together.

12. With ½" seam allowance, stitch through all layers and trim any fraying ends close.

13. Place cape over "shoulders" and secure with a little hot glue along inside frayed edge. Hold in place with a couple of quilt pins. (If these pinheads show, dab on a little black paint.)

14. Tuck the medallion under bow tie and hot glue in place.

THANKSGIVING THOUGHTS

For those of you who just have to have the traditional cornucopia on the dining table, this one's for you. This year, give the old tried and true a bit of a lift by raising the entire display up in a pedestal bowl. Ours is an antique silver one, but crystal or china would be equally as effective. Use a bit of dry foam by Floracraft to hold the leaves and grapes in place. And once you have the cornucopia complete, move on to the projects in this section—each sure to make you thankful of their ease and elegance each time you look at them.

More Mottled Leaves

AUTUMN FLAUNTS HER LEAVES IN AN IMPRESSIVE
ARRAY OF COLORS: REDS, ORANGES, YELLOWS,
RUSTS, EVEN FADING GREENS AND BROWNS. THERE'S
NO WAY TO REPLICATE HER PALETTE, BUT IT SURE IS
FUN TO TRY.

MATERIALS

- 1 large package #76 Cognac Fimo Modeling Clay
- 1 small package Fimo #42 Mandarin
- 1 small package Fimo #77 Terra Cotta
- 1 small package Fimo #16 Sunflower
- Very fine grater*
- Rolling pin or 2"-diameter round dowel about 1 foot long*

- X-Acto knife (or paring knife)*
- 1 pair thin disposable latex gloves
- Aluminum foil
- Cookie sheet
- 1 real leaf for every project leaf made, different sizes and heavily veined

*The grater, rolling pin, and knife should be dedicated to crafting and not used for food in the future.

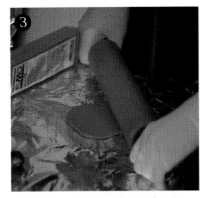

For each leaf:

1. Cover your working area and cookie sheet with aluminum foil.

2. Put on your latex gloves and break off 1½" of #76 Cognac Fimo. Crumble it and knead until soft and pliable.

3. Roll Fimo out until about ¼" thick, as shown at right.

4. With tiny grater, grate orange, yellow, and brown Fimo all over the rolled-out Cognac Fimo piece, as shown.

5. Place leaf, back-side down, onto rolled-out Fimo. Roll with rolling pin gently so leaf sticks to Fimo.

6. With knife, carefully cut around the edges of the leaf and remove excess Fimo and then carefully peel leaf from Fimo.

7. Place leaf on foil-lined cookie sheet. Use little pieces of rolled-up foil to add curves to your leaf, as shown below, thereby giving it a more natural appearance.

8. Bake according to directions on the Fimo package.

9. After baking, wash all utensils thoroughly, store grater, rolling pin, knife with craft materials, and throw away the gloves.

Detail of finished leaves.

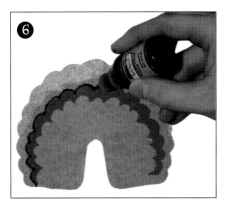

Paper-Tailed Pinecone Turkeys

MATERIALS

- 8½" x 11" sheet brown mottled cardstock
- 2-oz. bottle Ivory Delta Ceramcoat Acrylic Paint
- 2-oz. bottle Red Delta Ceramcoat Acrylic Paint
- 1 small Scribbles Shiny Black 3-D Paint
- 3 medium-sized pinecones
- Scissors
- 8½" x 11" sheet tracing paper
- Fine-tipped paintbrush
- 2" square art sponge
- Patterns (page 116)

MARK'S MOM SHOWED HIM HOW TO MAKE THESE WHEN HE WAS A LITTLE TYKE. AND EVERY YEAR, HIS FAMILY STILL MAKES THEM FOR THANKSGIVING. NOW YOU CAN SHARE IN THAT FAMILY TRADITION AND PERHAPS START A NEW ONE OF YOUR OWN.

1. Trace the patterns on page 116 onto tracing paper and then onto the brown cardstock; you will need three of each tail and head piece.

2. Cut the tail and head pieces out.

3. Use the paper pattern tail to cover all but the top ½" of the brown cardstock tailpiece and lightly sponge on the ivory paint.

4. Follow with a scalloped line of red paint.

5. Repeat steps 3 and 4 on the other two brown cardstock tailpieces.

6. When dry, outline red on top and bottom with black paint on each tailpiece, as shown at left.

7. On each brown headpiece, paint "gobble" red and dot on an eye.

8. Find out on which side the pinecone wants to "sit" without rolling, and add tail and head to top.

Wooden-Tailed Pinecone Turkeys

These little decorative turkeys are a simple but cute variation of the Paper-Tailed Pinecone Turkey project on the previous page. The wooden tails add a bit more durability to the finished project, making it easier to pack them away and display them year after year.

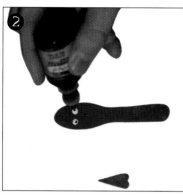

MATERIALS (PER TURKEY)

- 14 wooden ice cream spoons
- 1" wooden flowerpot
- 1" wooden heart
- 1 pair 2" wooden angel wings
- Medium-size pinecone
- 2-oz. bottle Medium Brown Delta Ceramcoat Acrylic Paint
- 2-oz. bottle Ivory Delta Ceramcoat Acrylic Paint
- 1 small Scribbles Shiny Black 3-D Paint
- 1 can rust-colored spray paint
- Paintbrush
- Hot glue gun and glue sticks

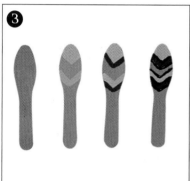

1. Paint one spoon solid brown and let dry.

2. Use ivory paint and a dot of black to create eyes, as shown at left. Let dry.

3. Using the photo at the left as your guide, paint tail in steps.

4. Paint heart with rust-colored spray paint.

5. Paint flowerpot black and paint on an ivory-colored square for buckle.

6. Paint angel wings, alternating brown and ivory paint, as shown. Allow to dry.

7. Hot glue heart with point facing up to front of solid brown spoon for the "gobble."

8. Hot glue flowerpot to top of spoon for pilgrim hat.

9. Give all pieces a very light spritz with the rust-colored spray paint.

10. Find out which way the pinecone won't roll and hot glue head spoon to top of pinecone, as shown.

11. Hot glue angel wing pieces to either side of the head on the body to serve as the turkey wings.

12. Hot glue the tail spoons in a fan to the back of the pinecone body, as shown below.

Pilgrim Girl Character Wreath®

HEARTH AND HOME WERE THE MOST PROMINENT
FEATURES IN A PILGRIM GIRL'S LIFE.
SUBSTITUTING FOR A 1600S PLYMOUTH SALTBOX
HOUSE IS THE NEWBURY PIONEER HOME AS
RECREATED AT THE STAGE COACH INN MUSEUM.

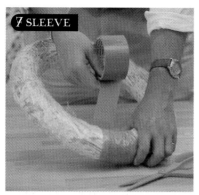
7 SLEEVE

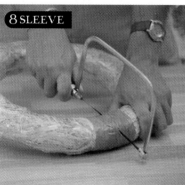
8 SLEEVE

8 SLEEVE

8 SLEEVE

- 14" straw wreath
- 5" to 6" vinyl doll with head
- ⅓-yard brown/beige checked fabric
- 1 yard crisp white muslin
- 3 wooden buttons
- 1 package quilt pins
- 12" wicker cornucopia
- 24 picks various autumn veggies, flora, and fauna
- Small handsaw
- Packing tape
- Floracraft dry foam brick
- 2 2"-long nails
- Iron
- Hot glue gun and glue sticks
- Needle
- Brown thread
- Drill and 1½" bit
- Patterns (page 116-117)
- Spray starch (optional)

For the head:

1. Remove head from doll body, if necessary, and set aside.

2. From white muslin, cut two caps, four cuffs, and two collars according to the patterns (pages 116-117). The collar is cut from the white muslin exactly the size of an 8½" x 11" sheet of paper with the front opening and neck hole cut from one side.

3. With ½" seam allowance and muslin cap pieces right sides together, stitch cap, leaving 2" turn opening on the back curve.

4. Clip cap corners, turn right-side out, and press.

5. Tightly hand-gather cap along back curve to stop lines.

6. Place cap on head. The brim should hang a bit in front of forehead. Use quilt pins to secure to vinyl doll head at the stop-stitch lines. Turn brim back. Set head aside once again.

For the sleeves:

1. Pin two muslin cuff pieces right sides together and with ½" seam allowance, stitch, leaving a 2" hole for turning near but never on a corner.

2. Clip cuff corners, turn, and press.

3. Repeat steps 1 and 2 for other cuff. Set aside.

4. With ½" seam allowance and right sides facing, stitch collar pieces together, leaving a 2" turn opening in the back.

5. Clip collar corners, turn, and press. Set aside.

6. With right sides together, stitch the ⅓-yard x 45" checked fabric into a tube. Set aside.

7. Cover about a 3" area of the wreath with packing tape, as shown top left.

8. Saw through wreath at center of taped area and use the packing tape to tightly wrap raw ends to keep straw from falling out, as shown in the progression of photos at left.

9. With drill and 1½" bit, bore hole in top of wreath opposite the saw cut, as shown at right. This is the head hole.

10. Slip checked fabric tube onto wreath.

11. Cut a slit in the sleeve at the top of the wreath to match the positioning of the head hole, fill hole with hot glue, and insert doll head. Hold until dry.

12. Put collar around neck, opening in front, and hot glue in an inconspicuous area to hold.

13. Add a wooden button to center of collar by first stitching through its holes with thread and then gluing it into place.

14. Wrap cuffs around wreath at "wrist" area. Hold in place with a bit of hot glue.

15. Stitch on a button through both sides of cuff to close, as shown at right.

9 SLEEVE

15 SLEEVE

Final touches:

Let's face it, the face is adorable, but it's that cornucopia that really makes this wreath worth looking at.

1. Attach cornucopia to the wreath's arms with 2" nails pushed through the wicker and sunk deep into the straw and secured with hot glue.

2. Fill the cornucopia with the dry foam brick held in place with hot glue.

3. Fill up the outside with leaves, berries, veggies, and flowers by starting with a "platform" of autumn leaves around the bottom that extends well past the mouth of the cornucopia.

4. Build up with grapes, gourds, and other veggies.

5. Fill gaps with small flowers, lots of berries, and more autumn leaves as you go.

Did You Know?
Pilgrims and Thanksgiving didn't always go hand in hand. It wasn't until the early 1900s that the Pilgrims became a staple character in our annual celebration.

PATTERNS AND ART

Green Goblins, Little
Witch Girl Doll, and
Trixie LeTreat Hat
Brim Patterns

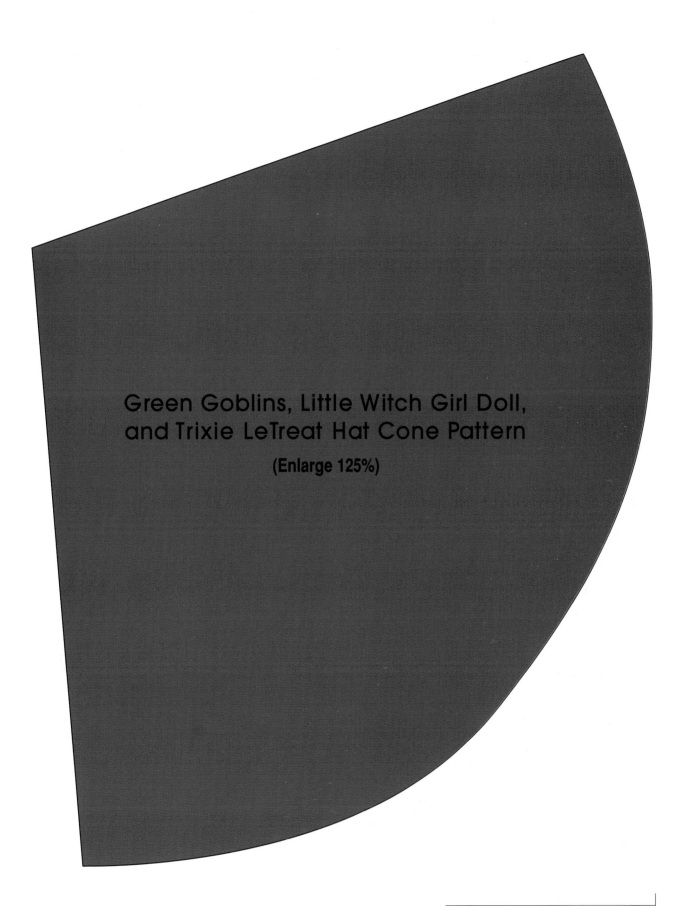

Green Goblins, Little Witch Girl Doll,
and Trixie LeTreat Hat Cone Pattern

(Enlarge 125%)

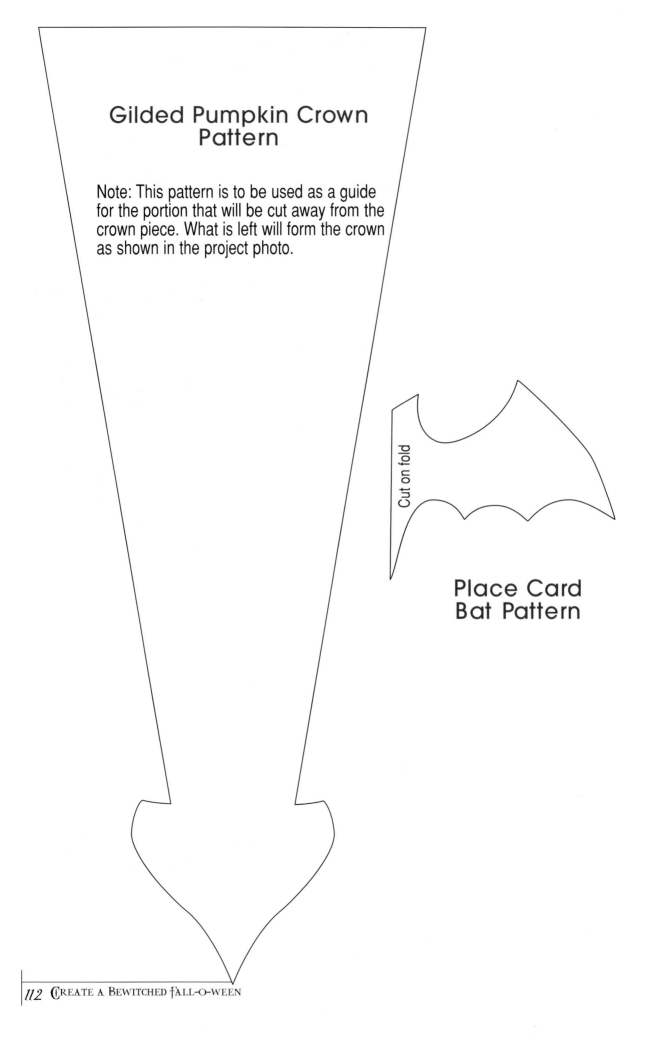

Gilded Pumpkin Crown
Pattern

Note: This pattern is to be used as a guide for the portion that will be cut away from the crown piece. What is left will form the crown as shown in the project photo.

Cut on fold

Place Card
Bat Pattern

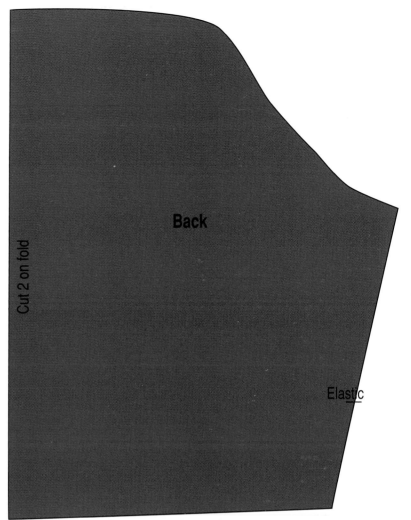

Back

Cut 2 on fold

Elastic

Place on eyelet border

Little Witch Girl Doll Bodice Patterns

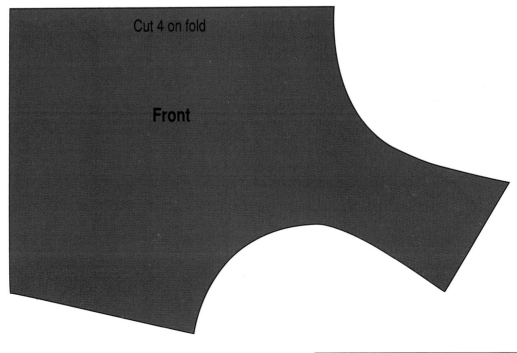

Cut 4 on fold

Front

Trixie LeTreat
Sleeve Pattern

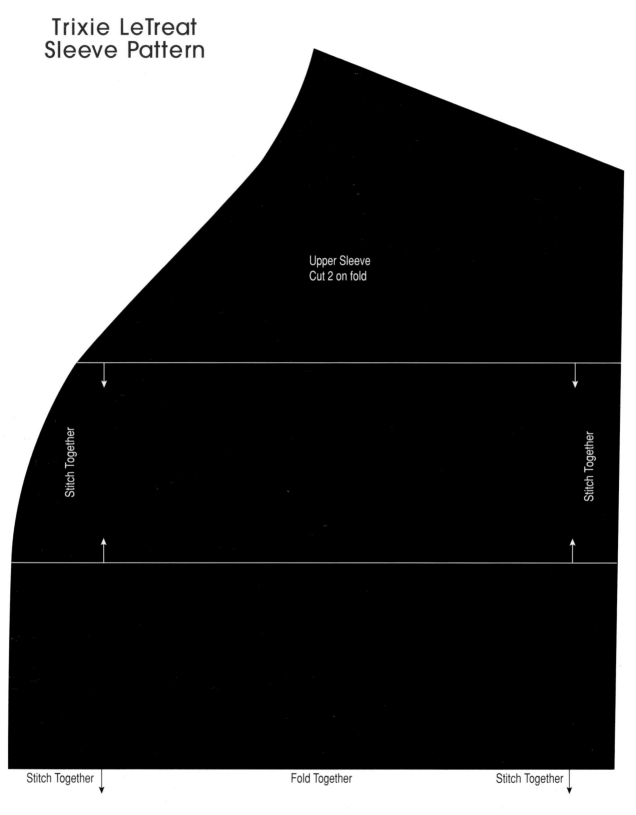

Upper Sleeve
Cut 2 on fold

Stitch Together

Stitch Together

Stitch Together

Fold Together

Stitch Together

(Enlarge 125%)

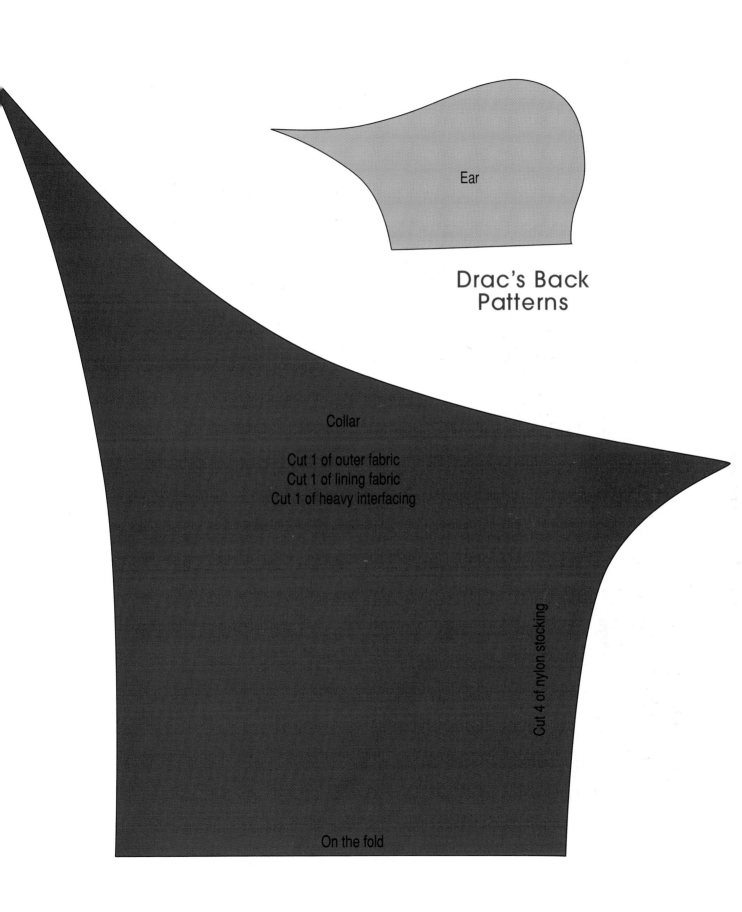

Ear

Drac's Back Patterns

Collar

Cut 1 of outer fabric
Cut 1 of lining fabric
Cut 1 of heavy interfacing

Cut 4 of nylon stocking

On the fold

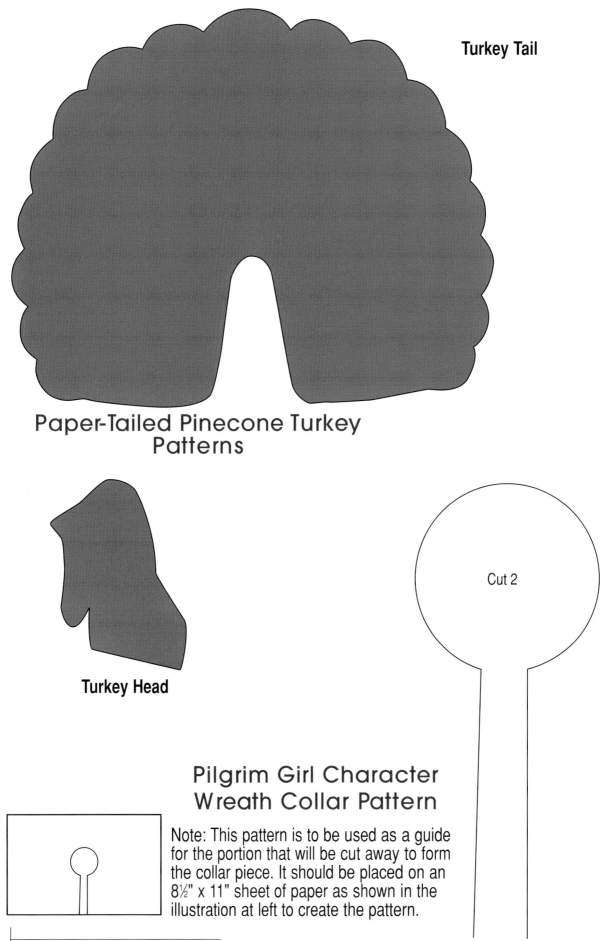

Turkey Tail

Paper-Tailed Pinecone Turkey Patterns

Turkey Head

Cut 2

Pilgrim Girl Character Wreath Collar Pattern

Note: This pattern is to be used as a guide for the portion that will be cut away to form the collar piece. It should be placed on an 8½" x 11" sheet of paper as shown in the illustration at left to create the pattern.

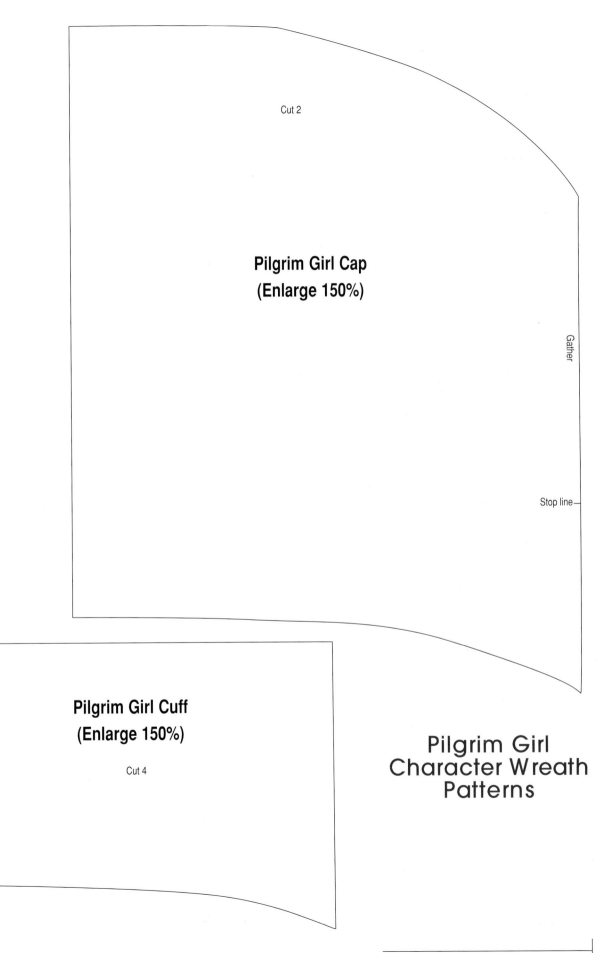

Cut 2

Pilgrim Girl Cap
(Enlarge 150%)

Gather

Stop line

Pilgrim Girl Cuff
(Enlarge 150%)

Cut 4

Pilgrim Girl Character Wreath Patterns

Paper Party Hats
and Clip Art Bats

Halloween Bed Sheets
Cat Art

Vintage Puddy-Tat Pillows
Cat Art

Vintage Puddy-Tat Pillows
Cat Art

MADE IN U. S A.

Copr H. E. Luhrs

RESOURCES

Most all of the products used in this book are easily accessible at stores such as JoAnn Fabrics and Crafts, Michael's Craft Stores, and Home Depot. However, if you need further assistance locating any of the products feel free to look up these wonderful suppliers either by phone or online.

Accent Import Export, Inc.
Phone: (800) 989-2889
www.fimozone.com
Fimo polymer clay.

Beistle Co.
Phone: (717) 532-2131
Products can be found in retail stores that sell holiday merchandise.

Christmas by Krebs, Corp.
P.O. Box 5730 R.I.A.C.
Roswell, NM 88202-5730
Fax: (505) 623-3034
Decorative glass balls.

Christopher Radko Collection
Phone: (800) 71-RADKO
www.christopherradko.com
Fine autumn, Halloween, and Thanksgiving figural glass ornaments.

Creative Beginnings
Phone: (800) 367-1739
Diamond Dust Glitter.

Dalen Products Inc.
Phone: (800) 747-3256
www.Gardeneer.com
Yard owls.

DAPtex Insulation Foam Sealant
Phone: (888) DAPTIPS

Delta Technical Coatings, Inc.
2550 Pellissier Place
Whittier, CA 90601
Phone: (800) 423-4135
RF Gold Foiling Kit #09910, RF Silver Foiling Kit #09920, Gold Foil #06 101, Silver Foil #06 102, and Adhesive # 06 402.

Designs by Dian
Phone: (417) 732-9030
www.diandolls.com
Great Santa masks and porcelain doll heads.

Dritz®
P.O. Box 5028
Spartanburg, SC 29304
Web site: www.dritz.com
Cheesecloth.

Faerie's Finest
Phone: (562) 983-8397
Fax: (240) 358-4321
www.faeriesfinest.com
e-mail: info@faeriesfinest.com
An online emporium of gourmet seasoning, distinctively flavored sugars and salts, gourmet cocoas, unique seasoning blends, herbs and spices, and the highest quality flavor extracts and oils.

Floracraft
www.floracraft.com

Graphic Products Corp.
Phone: (800) 323-1660
Fax: (847) 836-9666
e-mail:
GraphicProducts@aol.com
Black Ink Papers.

Hats by Leko
Phone: (800) 817-4287

Haunted Studio
Lewis Barrett Lehrman
www.HauntedStudio.com

Homer Laughlin China Co.
Phone: (800) 452-4462
www.Fiestawarefiesta.com
Fiestaware.

island*moon
Mandy Keefer
P.O. Box 736
Janesville, CA 96114
Phone: (530) 253-3006
e-mail: IslandMoonEssentials
@yahoo.com
http://members.ebay.com/
aboutme/island*moon/
Original hand-painted wooden signs.

Lazertran
Phone: (800) 245-7547
www.lazertran.com
Transfer papers.

Libbey®
Phone: (419) 325-2100
www.Libbey.com
Java Lava dinnerware.

MacJac Ent. L.L.C.
Phone: (480) 946-1828
Fax: (480) 946-1909
www.funkins.com
Fun-kins Artificial Pumpkins.
Modern Options® (a division
of Triangle Coating™)
e-mail:
info@modernoptions.com
www.modernoptions.com
Sophisticated Finishes™.

Mummert Sign Co.
Phone: (717) 259-8055

Papermart
Phone: (800) 745-8800
www.papermart.com
Storage boxes.

Plaid Enterprises
www.Plaidonline.com
Stiffy Fabric Stiffener.

Plastikote
Phone: (800) 328-8044
Fleck Stone and other paint
finishes.
Roses Doll House
Orders only: (800) 926-9093
www.doll@happyhobby.com
Dollhouse building supplies.

Rusty Tin-tiques
Decorator & Craft Corp.
428 Zelta
Wichita, KS 67207
Papier-mâché hatboxes.

Seasons Gone By
Phone: (877) 252-9085
Reproduction paper pulp
pumpkins and more.

Sugar Crafts
Phone: (513) 896-7089
e-mail:
proicer@sugarcraft.com
Candy Apple Magic Mix.

Tender Heart Treasures
Phone: (800) 443-1367
Fax: (402) 593-1316

Terry's Village
Phone: (800) 200-4400.
www.terrysvillage.com

Transylvania Imports
Phone: (310) VAMPIRE
www.vampire.com
Vampire Wine
(a.k.a. Pinot Grigio).

Van Dyke Supply Co., Inc.
Phone: (800) 787-3355
Pressure sensitive wooden
strips.

Stars of Halloween Revealed

The stars in those
childhood photos in the
Autumn Au-rrangements section,
page 28, are none other than
beloved "Bewitched" stars:
Elizabeth Montgomery (Samantha);
Marion Lorne (Aunt Clara);
Alice Ghostley (Esmeralda);
and Agnes Moorehead,
(Endora, Samantha's mother).